Reader's Digest

Vol. 130 No 778 February 1987

Editor-in-Chief: Michael Randolph
Deputy Editors: Lois Fletcher, Sheila Slater
Senior Editors: Katherine Walker, Julia Watson
Research Editor: Patricia Myers
Roving Editors: Peter Browne, John Ennis,
John Harman, David Moller
Assistant Editors: Veronica Pratt, Cathryn Stone
Associate Editor: Leslie Farrow
Excerpts Editor: Simon Firth
Sub-Editors: Olwen Fisher, Helen Powell,
Michael Bradley
Researchers: Nicola Cross, Lucy Wildman,
Jane de Zonie
Librarian: Patricia Hamer
Magazine Administrator: Joanna Cruddas

Art Editor: Ken Ellis
Assistant Art Editors: Christopher White, Diana Turner
Art Researcher: Patricia Hall

February Issue Editor: Julia Watson

Advertising
Senior Associate Director: Henry van Wyk
General Manager: Madeleine MacDonnell
Sales Managers: Stephen Marsh, Yvonne Richards
Media Services: David Luetchford
Marketing and Merchandising: Ian Aitken
Birmingham: Brian Taylor   *Edinburgh:* Peter Bailey

Sales
Subscriptions: Ann Paetke

Customer Services
Director: Mitchell Stockton,
7–10 Old Bailey, London EC99 1AA.
Subscriptions: UK £17·34 a year. Republic
of Ireland IR£20·00 a year. Overseas £25·00 a year.
All prices include delivery
British Reader's Digest is published by
THE READER'S DIGEST ASSOCIATION LTD
25 BERKELEY SQUARE, LONDON W1X 6AB
Managing Director: Neil McRae
Directors: Brian Gray, Richard Hewett, Robin Hosie,
Andrew Lynam-Smith, Michael Randolph,
Mitchell Stockton

READER'S DIGEST ASSOCIATION, INC (USA)
Founders: DeWitt Wallace and Lila Acheson Wallace
Editor-in-Chief: Kenneth O. Gilmore
Executive Editor, International: Jeremy H. Dole
Chairman and Chief Executive Officer: George V. Grune

COVER PICTURE "Royal Ballet Student"
Robert Heindel has been called "the Degas of our
time." This painting is one of a series, the fruit of
two years spent observing, sketching and
photographing the dancers of the Royal Ballet.
The resulting works, in oil and pastel, were
shown in a successful 1985 exhibition at the
Royal Festival Hall.

Squadron Leader Warwick
Woodhouse of Richmond, North
Yorkshire, is one of the readers
who sent in a **Humour in Uniform**
story (see page 51). Do *you*
have a true story, from your own
experience, that shows the funny
side of service life? Write and tell
us in your own words. We pay
£100 for every story accepted.

We also offer £100 for
Life's Like That stories—the
funny side of everyday life—and
for **College Rags** (page 127).

For other short items and
end-of-article "fillers" we pay
from £25 upwards.

All payments are made on acceptance.
Write to:

> **Excerpts, Reader's Digest,**
> **25 Berkeley Square,**
> **London W1X 6AB**

Make sure your name and address
appear on all items.

We regret that we cannot acknowledge
or return contributions, or accept
responsibility for loss or damage.

Changing your address?
Please use the coupon on page 18.

ENJOY LIFE WITH A
REGULAR MONTHLY INCOME

INCOME BONDS.
Probably the most enjoyable investment you'll ever make.

An investment in National Savings Income Bonds will give you the money you need to enjoy life, month in, month out.

The interest rate on Income Bonds is 12·25% p.a.*

You'll receive your income monthly and in full, because we don't deduct tax at source.

The interest is credited direct to your bank or building society account on the 5th of each month, or we can send it direct to your home.

Either way it means some welcome money coming in regularly.

No need to touch your capital.

You get your monthly income without needing to touch your capital.

Interest is calculated on a day-to-day basis. It is paid in full and is subject to tax if you are a taxpayer.

The rate paid may change from time to time, to keep it competitive.

Getting your money out.

You can have your bonds repaid at 3 months' notice. And there will be no loss of interest if you've held your bonds for a year or more. (For full details of repayment, see the prospectus.)

This is what 12·25%* p.a. earns you every month:

INVESTMENT	AVERAGE MONTHLY INCOME	INVESTMENT	AVERAGE MONTHLY INCOME
£2,000	£20	£ 15,000	£ 153
£5,000	£51	£ 25,000	£ 255
£8,000	£81	£100,000	£1,020

(Each additional £1,000 invested produces an average of £10 a month – £122 a year. Maximum holding £100,000.

*Interest rate correct at time of going to press. To check the rate phone 0800 100 100 (any time) free.

What to do.

For a prospectus and further details complete the coupon and send it to: National Savings FREEPOST 4335, Bristol BS1 3YX.

Full details are also available at post offices or you can ring 0800 100 100 (any time) free.

The minimum purchase for new investors is £2,000; if you already have a bond, it is £1,000.

It Pays to Enrich Your Word Power

BY PETER FUNK

EVEN in the computer age, you need a way with words. In the following list, tick the word or phrase you believe is *nearest in meaning* to the key word. Answers are on the next page.

(1) **schema** (SKEE muh)—A: forecast. B: stage curtain. C: inventory. D: diagram.

(2) **pugnacious**—A: plain. B: stubborn. C: quarrelsome. D: conciliatory.

(3) **consolation**—A: expectation. B: comfort. C: prolonged discussion. D: well-being.

(4) **farrago** (fuh RAH go)—A: old-fashioned game. B: worthless object. C: mixture. D: foolishness.

(5) **boggle**—A: to hesitate. B: coax. C: sink into. D: reassure.

(6) **intrusive**—A: instinctive. B: frustrating. C: patronizing. D: interfering.

(7) **lineaments** (LIN ee ah ments)—A: characteristics. B: boundaries. C: sports equipment. D: medicinal products.

(8) **staunch**—A: cantankerous. B: virile. C: trustworthy. D: indecisive.

(9) **communiqué** (kuh MEW nǐ kay)—A: propaganda. B: translation. C: announcement. D: intimation.

(10) **legacy**—A: gift from a will. B: epic tale. C: business contract. D: judge's ruling.

(11) **minion** (MIN yun)—A: oblivion. B: servant. C: minor character. D: young person.

(12) **propound**—A: to talk at length. B: perplex. C: propose. D: argue.

(13) **burnish**—A: to scorch. B: roughen. C: stain. D: polish.

(14) **portable**—capable of being A: drunk safely. B: floated. C: flexible. D: carried.

(15) **sleazy** (SLEE zee)—A: slippery. B: shiftless. C: shoddy. D: foolish.

(16) **moil**—A: procedure. B: hard work. C: environment. D: something central.

(17) **disrupt**—A: to throw into disorder. B: anger. C: unwrap. D: toss out.

(18) **omniscient** (om NIS ee ent, om NISH yent)—A: all-powerful. B: present everywhere. C: knowing everything. D: extremely popular.

(19) **giddy**—A: dizzy. B: distracted. C: unreasonable. D: infatuated.

(20) **exiguous** (eg ZIG you us, ig ZIG you us)—A: precise. B: easy. C: near-by. D: scanty.

Answers to

It Pays to Enrich Your Word Power

(1) **schema**—D: Diagram; outline; synopsis. Greek *skhēma* (form, figure).

(2) **pugnacious**—C: Quarrelsome; eager to fight. Latin *pugnare* (to fight).

(3) **consolation**—B: Comfort at a time of grief, disappointment or the like. Latin *consolari*.

(4) **farrago**—C: Mixture; hotchpotch; as, a *farrago* of political ideas. Latin (mixed fodder).

(5) **boggle**—A: To hesitate or demur. Also, to be startled or baffled. Probably from Scottish *bogle* (spectre).

(6) **intrusive**—D: Interfering; pushing or forcing oneself into or upon without invitation or welcome. Latin *in-* and *trudere* (to thrust).

(7) **lineaments**—A: Distinctive characteristics; as, to sketch the broad *lineaments* of Lebanon's difficulties. Also, facial features. Latin *linea* (line).

(8) **staunch**—C: Trustworthy; unwavering; loyal. "He is a *staunch* believer in human rights." Old French *estanche* (watertight).

(9) **communiqué**—C: Announcement; official communication; report. French (communicated).

(10) **legacy**—A: Gift of property or money as stated in a will; bequest. Also something passed down by a predecessor; as, a former government's *legacy* of high taxes. Latin *legare* (to bequeath).

(11) **minion**—B: Servant; favourite; servile agent; as, the *minions* of Louis XIV. Old French *mignot*.

(12) **propound**—C: To propose; put forward for consideration; as, to *propound* a new theory of the universe. Latin *proponere* (to set forth).

(13) **burnish**—D: To polish by rubbing; as, to *burnish* a silver tray. Old French *burnir* (to make brown).

(14) **portable**—D: capable of being carried; easily movable. Latin *portare* (to carry).

(15) **sleazy**—C: Shoddy; squalid; slatternly. Origin uncertain.

(16) **moil**—B: Hard work; drudgery; as, the *moil* of processing endless forms. Also, confusion and turmoil. Old French *moillier* (to moisten).

(17) **disrupt**—A: To throw into disorder; shatter; break in pieces. Latin *dis-* (apart) and *rumpere* (to break).

(18) **omniscient**—C: Knowing everything; having very extensive knowledge. "Little children believe parents are *omniscient*." Latin *omni* (all) and *scire* (to know).

(19) **giddy**—A: Dizzy; excitable; lightheaded; whatever causes this feeling; as, *giddy* heights. Also, frivolous; flighty; as, *giddy* teenagers. Old English *gidig* (insane).

(20) **exiguous**—D: Scanty; small; as, the *exiguous* income of the African peasant farmer. Latin *exiguus*.

Vocabulary Ratings

20-19 correct .... excellent
18-16 correct .... good
15-14 correct .... fair

Dimplex makes electric home heating look better than ever.

The latest Dimplex storage heaters combine exceptional slimness with a controllability never before achieved.

The Dimplex XTE Supertronic is less than six inches deep, yet it's more efficient than older storage heaters twice the thickness. But here's a difference. Each XTE Supertronic storage heater comes with its own separate 'brain', a unique temperature sensor that reads the temperature at night and uses that reading to judge how much heat will be needed the following day. So, if the weather changes the heater automatically adjusts itself to meet the change.

So, not only does the Dimplex Supertronic run on Economy 7 low price electricity – less than half price compared with the standard domestic rate – it uses it very efficiently as well. The result is more comfort and lower running costs. That's why you'll find that Dimplex storage heating can be the cheapest way of heating in many homes.

For further details send in the coupon or ring 01-200 0200.

When you've got a friend who comes to dinner every day, how do you ring the changes?

If you've got a friend who's rather particular about food, the chances are, it's your cat.

Cats really can distinguish between the different varieties.

And that's why the Whiskas range offers a wider choice than any other canned cat food.

In fact, with 14 appetising varieties, there's a different one for every day of the week – and the week after that.

And because each perfectly balanced Whiskas recipe has its own distinctive taste, texture and smell, you can be sure your little friend will always be back to see what's on the menu for tea.

whiskas

MORE CATS THAN EVER BEFORE
NOW PREFER WHISKAS.

Personal Glimpses

ACTOR Paul Eddington, star of *Yes, Prime Minister*, says he has grown so much into the role of a politician that he finds himself saying, "I am warming to the principle," when a simple "yes" would suffice. —Reuters

MANY years ago, I attended a star-studded charity gala at the old Madison Square Garden in New York.

Presently the band struck up the opening chords of "The Star-Spangled Banner." As we rose to our feet, I noticed a woman a few feet away lift one hand in the air and start to wave. *How rude!* I thought. *Why is she trying to call attention to herself during the national anthem?*

Then I realized who she was. Rather than trying to disrupt the proceedings, she seemed intent on joining in the praise of her nation. The movements of her fingers and the radiant smile that highlighted her face were Helen Keller's glorious "voice." —Naomi Lawrence

KINGSLEY AMIS describes his methods of overcoming writer's block:

Writing every day, seven days a week—that's very important, even if it's only ten lines, because then the unconscious stays interested. The other thing is—for writing purposes as well as cleanliness—have a shower or bath every day, because you've got to occupy your attention. You're not just sitting there thinking of nothing but writing—there's something else going on. Shaving is ideal. That keeps things in trim: the unconscious stays interested, because it's getting a regular outing. —*Writer's Block* (BBC Radio 4)

A FRIEND of the Soviet physicist and dissident Andrei Sakharov tells this story:

A year before Russian authorities sent him into exile, some friends were holidaying with the Sakharovs on the Black Sea. Once they jokingly asked his wife, Elena, what Sakharov thought about while strolling along the waterfront. They suggested that he was contemplating violations of the Helsinki Accords. "Nonsense!" she said, laughing. "Here, in this romantic setting, he thinks only of me."

That evening they were all walking along the harbour as the palm trees rustled and the stars twinkled. "Ask

9

him," whispered Elena, anticipating her triumph.

"Andrei," they cautiously enquired, "what are you thinking about?"

"Radiation in outer space," was his reply.
— Vassily Aksyonov

PETER USTINOV recalls his early days as an actor:

I went to a drama school where we had to be animals for one whole term. Most of the ambitious girls became gazelles and swallows, exhausting themselves for little purpose. The boys preferred virile creatures like tigers. Being lazy by conviction as well as by nature, I became a salamander, and lay perfectly still for four months, an expression of glazed surprise on my face, occasionally flicking my tongue to show I was alive.
— quoted by Fleur Cowles in *People as Animals* (Robin Clark)

DUKE ELLINGTON had been developing and honing the sound for ten years by the time swing became a worldwide phenomenon, so he, more than anyone else, had a right to be discouraged when the music became identified with white stars. Yet, even in disappointment, the Duke was the most dignified of men. "I took the energy it takes to pout," he said, "and wrote some blues."
— Ted Fox, *Showtime at the Apollo* (Quartet Books)

POP star Cliff Richard remembers a visit to one of the Bihari refugee camps in Bangladesh:

That first morning I must have washed my hands a dozen times. I didn't want to touch anything, least of all the people. Everyone in those camps, even the babies, was covered in sores and scabs.

I was bending down to one little mite, mainly for the photographer's benefit, and trying hard not to have too close a contact, when someone accidentally stood on the child's fingers. He screamed out and, as a reflex, I grabbed hold of him, forgetting all about his dirt and his sores. I remember now that warm little body clinging to me and the crying instantly stopped. In that moment I knew I had an enormous amount to learn about practical Christian loving, but that at least I'd started.

The photograph of me standing ashen-faced with that little boy buried in my shoulder is one of my most treasured possessions. It hangs on the wall between my bedroom and bathroom, where I can't fail to see it or remember it.
— *Which One's Cliff?* (Hodder & Stoughton)

THE Queen Mother has always had an instinctive ability to do and say precisely what is needed.

On her wedding day at Westminster Abbey in 1923, before she walked up the lengthy aisle, she placed her wedding bouquet on the grave of the Unknown Warrior in front of her. When her horse Devon Loch stumbled within sight of the winning-post in the 1956 Grand National, her first thought was for the jockey and her stable: "I must go down and comfort those poor people." And at Frogmore in 1972, beside the Duke of Windsor's grave, when his widow was distraught, it was the Queen Mother who took the Duchess's arm gently and said: "I know how you feel. I've been through it myself."
— Alastair Burnet, *The ITN Book of the Queen Mother* (Michael O'Mara Books)

We pay £25 or more for "Personal Glimpse" anecdotes. See page 1.

Reader's Digest

FREE ENQUIRY SERVICE

Use this page to get any further information being offered by advertisers in this issue. Fill in the code numbers of the advertisers you wish to hear from (they are all listed overleaf); print your name and address, tear out this page, fold it as indicated and post it. No stamp is needed.

- - - - - - - THIRD FOLD HERE AND TUCK IN - - - - - - -

2

FIRST FOLD HERE

- - - - - - - SECOND FOLD HERE - - - - - - -

Please have information from the following advertisers sent to me:

Enter the code numbers from the list overleaf in these boxes

MR/MRS./MISS/MS ....

ADDRESS ....

....

....

POSTCODE

FEB 87

We regret that we are unable to fulfil overseas enquiries

Coupon valid until 31/7/87

USE THIS PAGE TO GET FURTHER INFORMATION FROM ADVERTISERS

This page is provided as a free service to you so that you can get further information from advertisers without cutting into your magazine. Fill in the coupon overleaf, tear out the whole page, fold it as indicated and post it. **No stamp is needed as postage is paid.**

To order any of the following:

Basketweave Jumper
Knitting Kit £29.95 24
Order direct from Ehrman, Freepost, London W8 4AA. (No stamp needed.)

Securikit £17.95 81
Four Super Paintbrushes
£4.50 126

Fill in the coupon overleaf, tear out the page, attach a cheque/PO (payable to Reader's Digest) and post, in an envelope, to
Reader Enquiry Service, 25 Berkeley Square, London W1X 6AB.

Send your donation direct to:
The Friedreich's Ataxia Group 125

Does Your English Let You Down?

By Richard G. Bagshaw

A SIMPLE technique for acquiring a swift mastery of good English has just been announced. It can double your powers of self-expression. It can pay you real dividends in business and social advancement, and give you added poise, self-confidence and greater personal effectiveness.

The details of this method are described in a fascinating book, "Good English—the Language of Success," sent free on request.

WHAT THIS FREE BOOK WILL SHOW YOU

How to stop making embarrassing mistakes in English!

How to become a fluent conversationalist and effective public speaker!

How to increase your vocabulary!

How to read faster and better!

How to put punch into your writing!

How to pass English examinations!

How to develop self-confidence!

How to increase your thinking power!

Influence

Many people do not realise how much they could influence others simply by speaking and writing with greater power, authority and precision. Whether you are presenting a report, training a child, fighting for a cause, making a sale, writing an essay, or asking for a rise . . . your success depends upon the words you use. Yet thousands of talented, intelligent people are held back because their powers of self-expression do not equal their other abilities.

Respect

But now the right words are yours to command! Never again need you fear those embarrassing mistakes. You can quickly and easily be shown how to ensure that everything you say and write is crisp, clear, *correct*. You can enormously increase your vocabulary, speed up your reading, enhance your powers of conversation, and greatly improve your grammar, writing and speaking. What's more, good English commands respect. It can help you to cut through many barriers to social, academic, and business success.

Free

To acquaint all readers with this easy-to-follow method for developing mastery of English, we, the publishers, have printed full details in a fascinating book, "Good English—the Language of Success," which will be sent free on request. No obligation. No need to even stamp your envelope. Simply write to: Practical English Programme (Dept. RGE9), FREEPOST 38, London W1E 6QZ.

Save money.
Think of your hot water tank
as a flask, not a kettle.

Sad but true. Some people see their hot water tank as a giant electric kettle.

They switch it on and off, on and off, as and when they need it.

They think they've got things under control. Until they realise they could have been getting a lot more for their money. And then they boil over.

Other people happily are not so short-sighted. To them, their hot water tank is a highly efficient thermos flask standing in the airing cupboard.

They think they've got things under control too. And they're right.

By changing to the Economy 7 tariff and heating their water on the cheap night rate,

they're getting their hot water for less than half price compared with the standard domestic rate.

Like a flask, a properly insulated water tank keeps the water you've heated overnight good and hot for when it's needed.

So when the bill arrives, the surprise is always a pleasant one.

And the most efficient way to switch from kettle to flask is just as painless. An Economy 7 system is designed to make the most of the cheap Economy 7 electricity, available for seven hours every night.

The special Economy 7 controller looks after your hot water automatically, switching on the heater in your flask (sorry, tank) every night for plenty of hot water the next day.

And if you happen to run out, you can always switch on the boost heater at the appropriate day rate.

It will automatically turn off again after an hour.

To make doubly sure your hot water stays piping hot, one of the latest Economy 7 high performance cylinders is recommended.

These tanks are 'super insulated' at the factory to keep in the heat.

By fitting an Economy 7 system you simply can't lose.

It'll look after your water heating requirements and save you money into the bargain.

Think about it. And if the idea of filling the flask instead of putting the kettle on makes sense to you, fill in the coupon for more details or a free survey from your local Electricity Board. Or dial 100 and ask for Freefone BuildElectric.

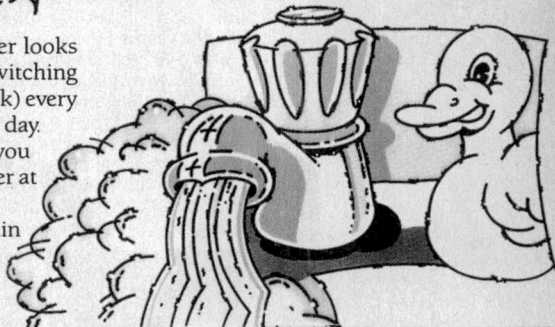

HINTS FOR YOUR HOME

Whether you're buying a new home or refurbishing your present one, you'll find some useful products here. Use the coupon on page 11 to get any further information you require. There are two more pages – 18 and 20.

Soften the hard lines of modern, functional architecture or create the period of your choice—medieval, classical Georgian, Adam style, Louis XIV or Victorian—by adding **Allied Guilds** ornamental plasterwork. Having specialised in its manufacture, fixing and restoration since the mid-1920's, Allied Guilds *guarantee genuine craftsmanship*. All their products are hand-made using the traditional ingredients of Plaster of Paris, Hessian and specially seasoned wood, yet they are easily fixed by d-i-y enthusiasts. Free illustrated brochure **360** on coupon on page 11.

Get rid of gaps between walls and kitchen worktops or baths easily and elegantly with **OBO Seals**. These are *not* mastic sealants, but rigid plastic strips that provide a tight seal against both wall and worktop to *prevent dirt and water seeping through*. The Kitchen Worktop Seal is available in 6 attractive finishes and the Bath Seal is made in 15 popular shades. Both can be brought from Texas, Payless, Great Mills, Madeleys and other leading DIY stores. For a free colour leaflet put **368** on the coupon on page 11.

Have your bedroom individually made for you by **Sharps** Bedrooms and not only will it look elegant, but you'll bless it for its tidiness. A Sharps bedroom is planned with you in your own home by one of their designers, then it's craftsman-built in their own factories and fitted by Sharps experts—usually in a day. You're dealing *direct* with the manufacturers so the cost is far less than you'd expect and regular special offers by Sharps give you even better value for your money. Get a Sharps brochure and the name of your nearest showroom by phoning 0800-555666. Or **370.**

Decorating the outside walls of your house is one of those expensive, time consuming jobs that come round far too quickly. But there is a way to avoid having to have it done again for at least 15 years! **Wallcote's** experts apply a tough, textured coating to form a permanent bond that will not flake, chip or peel—and it's *guaranteed*—for 15 years! And, according to an independent laboratory using BSI test methods, Wallcote will still be protecting your property 30 years hence! for details of a free survey phone 01-202 0933. Or **372** on coupon.

Carpets are a big investment so you want them to last. The **Duralay** *Book of Carpets and Carpet Care* tells you how to get the most out of your carpets. That means starting with the right underlay, one that will give the 'life support' your carpet needs. Duralay make a wide range of underlays and this booklet explains where you should use each type. It also tells you what to look for when buying carpets, what type to put where, and it explains pile and fibre types, tells you about carpet fitting and how to deal with accidental spills. For a free copy put **365** on the coupon, page 11

Super-efficient insulation is possible in *any* loft, no matter how irregularly spaced the joists, with **Micafil**. This natural, safe way to insulate your home couldn't be easier to install—you just pour it straight from the bag between the joists and level off. Ideal for first-time insulation and for topping up old insulation, Micafil creates an instant, self-sealing, heat-resistant barrier that leaves no gaps or space. Fibre-free, non-irritant and safe, it won't ride up, tear, crack, gape, burn, settle, cause dry rot or damage electrical wiring. Leaflet and stockists' names on coupon **367**, page 11.

A ROMANTIC EVENING WITH THE GAS CENTRAL HEATING BOILER.

It sounds unlikely, doesn't it? But, as you can see, a Baxi Bermuda is unlike any ordinary boiler. For a start the boiler itself is tucked away right out of sight in the chimney breast. (Saving you valuable space but nevertheless still powerful enough to heat up to ten radiators and gallons of hot water!)

In front there's an integral yet entirely independent gas fire, which you can use with or without the central heating. The Bermuda GF in the picture has real living flames, and will even light up to glow cosily when all the heat is off. It's only one of a range of seven modern and traditional designs to choose from.

Send us the coupon and we'll send you a colour brochure showing the full range of Baxi Bermudas. You too could fall in love with one of them.

(P.S. If you've got a Baxi Bermuda, installed since 1975, you could change just the gas fire front. Tick the box in the coupon for details.)

BAXI BERMUDA FIRESIDE CENTRAL HEATING

Please send me a Baxi Bermuda brochure.

Name _____

Address _____

Telephone _____

I am installing a new system ☐   I wish to replace an existing Bermuda fire front ☐   (Tick the appropriate box)

Send to: Baxi heating, Bamber Bridge, Preston. PR5 6SN   **RD2**

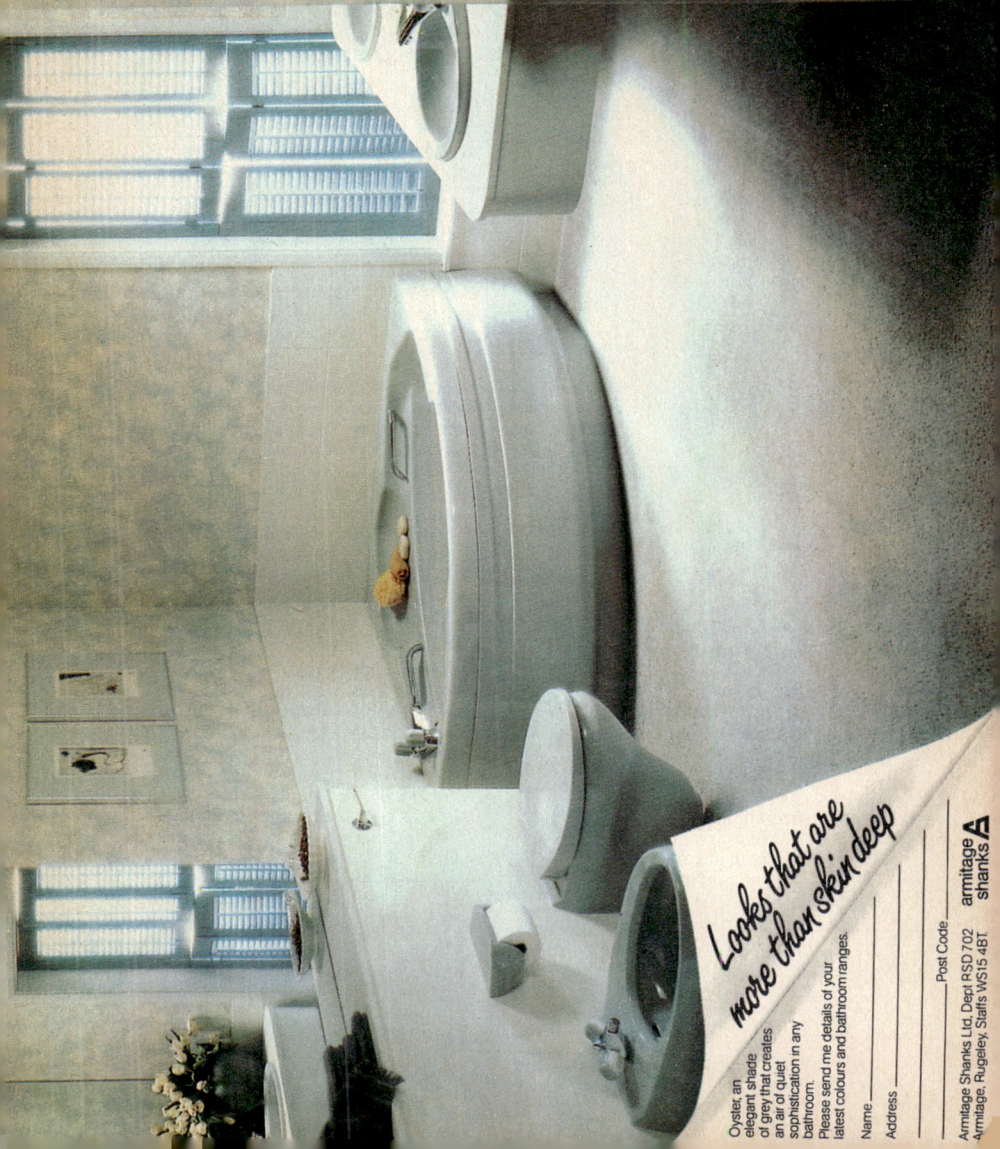

armitage shank
the bathroom

Looks that are
more than skin deep

Oyster, an
elegant shade
of grey that creates
an air of quiet
sophistication in any
bathroom.

Please send me details of your
latest colours and bathroom ranges.

Name _____

Address _____

Post Code _____

Armitage Shanks Ltd, Dept RSD 702
Armitage, Rugeley, Staffs WS15 4BT.

armitage
shanks △

HINTS FOR YOUR HOME

There's something to improve every home, large and small, here. Use the coupon that you'll find on page 11 to get any further information.

Renowned for their fitted kitchen furniture for many years, **Winchmore** have now added fitted *bedroom* furniture. Beautiful oak or maple, painted and laminate ranges, see all of it at your local *Winchmore Studio* where you'll get lots of expert free advice (no high pressure salesmen) and the offer of free plans and a quotation. Finance is also readily available at selected studios. Speedily installed by Winchmore trained fitters, their furniture is fully guaranteed. For a catalogue and location of your nearest Studio put **373** (kitchen) or **374** (bedroom) on the coupon.

Food waste can attract flies and cause bad odours in your kitchen. You shouldn't suffer from either one, *and* you'll have fewer trips to the rubbish bin, with an **In-Sink-Erator** because raw waste is ground up and flushed down the drain *instantly*. ISE is the world's No.1 disposer manufacturer (25 million units in use worldwide!) and they make a variety of models each one of which grinds down all food waste including nut shells, bones, tea leaves and potato peelings. For a free colour leaflet showing the ISE range put **366** on the coupon.

Hard water is hard on your heating costs—and hard on you! It builds up scale in pipes and hot water cylinders which causes fuel bills to build up. It also means scum and stains on baths and basins and rough treatment for you and your clothes. The answer is the gentle touch of a **Permutit Water Softener**. Quickly and easily plumbed into your home, it costs much less than you would imagine to achieve a softness in your household water that will be kinder to your skin, hair and clothes. Your pocket will enjoy the gentler touch, too. Details **369**.

"Move up please" is the message for anyone who is thinking of moving home to gain extra living space for a growing family. **Crescourt** will convert your loft for you with the minimum of fuss. Not only will this save you the upheaval of moving, but it'll be less costly *and* it'll add to the value of your home. Crescourt are professionals with over 16,000 conversions to their credit and they can arrange everything for you. They'll obtain planning permission and they can arrange finance, too (written quotation on request). Free brochure **364** on coupon, page 11.

Display your favourite china, a trophy or a flower arrangement on the wall! It'll look stunning in an **Aristocast** wall niche which can be fitted to any wall quickly and easily. Craftsman-made in attractive-looking traditional fibrous plaster, an Aristocast niche costs considerably less than one manufactured on site by a plasterer and there are 10 designs to choose from, including one for a corner. Complete fixing instructions are sent with every order and it's delivered to you by Aristocast's own transport. Free, full colour brochure **361**.

Suit your home and your needs to perfection with the addition of a **Banbury Conservatory**. The spacious *Victoriana* is one of a range that recreate the elegance of bygone times, or you can choose one of their many modern designs. All of them are built in the strongest, most resilient materials (including specially toughened glass) so they'll stay weather-proof and maintenance free for years. Banbury will advise you on finance, planning and installation, too, free of charge. They can also offer a personal loan at highly attractive interest rates. For free colour brochure call (0295) 811196 (24 hrs). Or **362** on coupon.

Laughter, the Best Medicine

A MINISTER was speaking to the Sunday school about the things money can't buy. "It can't buy laughter and it can't buy love," he told them. Driving his point home, he said, "What would you do if I offered you a thousand pounds not to love your mother and father?"

Stunned silence ensued. Finally, a small voice queried, "How much would you give me not to love my big sister?" —James Dent

MY WIFE said to me one day, "I met a fellow in town this morning, and right away I knew he was a trouble-maker. He started to insult me. He used bad language, even threatened me."

"How did you meet this fellow?" I asked, concerned.

And she told me: "I hit him with the car." —B. Meck in *Midnight Globe*

AN OLD miser called his doctor, lawyer and vicar to his death-bed. "They say you can't take it with you," the dying man said. "But I'm going to try. I've got three envelopes with £15,000 cash in each one. I want each of you to take an envelope, and just when they lower my coffin, you throw them in."

At the funeral each man tossed in his envelope. On the way home, the vicar confessed, "I needed money for the church, so I took out £5,000 and threw only £10,000 into the grave."

The doctor said, "I, too, must confess. I'm rebuilding my surgery. I took £10,000 and threw in only £5,000."

The lawyer said, "Gentlemen, I'm ashamed of you. I threw in a cheque for the full amount." —J.S.

"MAY I borrow your record-player to-night?" a man asked his neighbour.

"Certainly. Do you want to listen to some music?"

"No," the man answered. "Tonight I want to have some peace and quiet." —*Shin Min Daily News*, Singapore

A NEWLY landed Martian walked into a gambling casino and stood in front of a slot-machine, completely fascinated. He watched the dials spin round and was startled when a shower of silver coins came out. "Really," he said to the machine, "with a cold like that you should be in bed." —Gene Brown

We pay £25 or more for a joke for "Laughter, the Best Medicine." See page 1.

Anyone can offer you a warranty.

Many manufacturers will offer to sell you extended warranties when you buy a new car. Ford is no exception. We actually give you a choice of two. Extra Cover or Extra Cover Plus.

If you choose the latter, you'll get probably the best protection available for anything up to three years. Because,

not only does it cover literally hundreds of parts, but it also provides RAC membership for your new car.

This includes the full RAC Recovery Service. So, if you have a serious breakdown, or you're immobilised by an accident, you can have you and your car transported anywhere you

But will it come to your aid at 3am on a Sunday?

choose on the UK mainland.

Even if you break down at 3am on a Sunday morning help will be at hand.

You are also entitled to the RAC's At Home Service which means you're also covered if your car refuses to start on your own driveway.

And, best of all, once you've bought Extra Cover Plus none of this will cost you a penny.

So, when you're ordering the extras for your new Ford, don't forget Extra Cover Plus. It's one of the best options in the book.

Ford Service

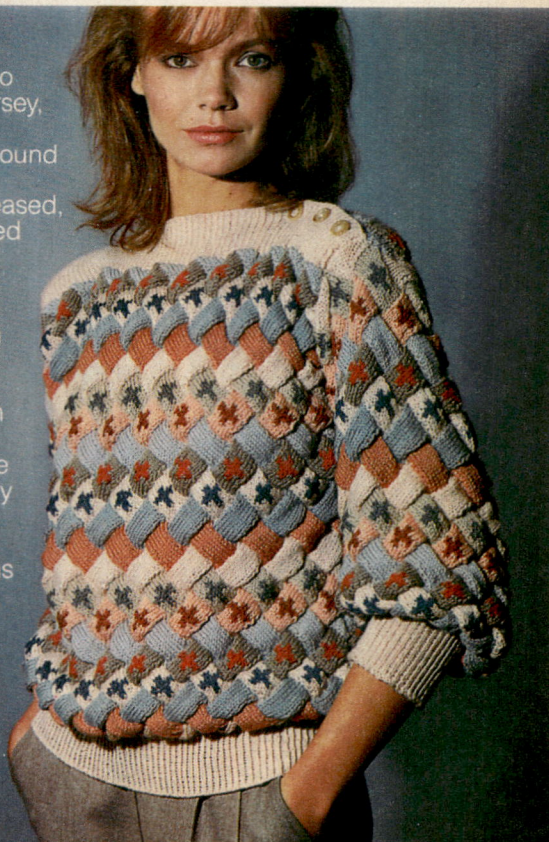

Ways of the World

THE week before Valentine's Day, a San Francisco dry-cleaning company cleans all red garments for half-price. And what do they do with the money they take in on red clothing? They donate it to the Heart Association.

—Virginia Leach

SULTAN Sir Muda Hassanal Bolkiah of Brunei rules one of the world's smallest independent countries (2,226 square miles), but his new 1,788-room palace on a hill overlooking the capital, Bandar Seri Begawan, is believed to be the largest royal residence in the world.

Costing an estimated £250 million, the palace comprises four interconnecting three-storey buildings that have a floor area of 25 acres. Topped by two domes encased in gold leaf, they are the centre-piece of a landscaped garden standing on a site of 350 acres. This magnificence—with four thrones in case a foreign king and queen come calling—is the tiny nation's seat of power.

—Robert Trumbull in *The New York Times*

EVERY day, during part of winter, the tiny mountain village of Orasso, Italy, has two sunrises and two sunsets. The phenomenon occurs because of the shape of a near-by 6,500-foot mountain.

Mount Riga has two humps, separated by wide dips. When the sun first comes up, it appears over one of the troughs. Around noon it disappears behind the first peak, bringing on the first sunset, and lights go on all over Orasso. The sun reappears when it reaches the second trough, prompting cockerels to crow a second time. When it hits the second hump in late afternoon, the sun vanishes for the night. —Nino Lo Bello

BEARDS, once a sacred part of Russian dress, have been declared unhygienic by the Soviet newspaper *Trud*, which encouraged citizens to shave them off.

The trade unions' newspaper quoted researchers at the Soviet Academy of Medical Science as saying that beards and big moustaches collect germs that are sucked into the lungs.

Thick beards are still worn by all Russian Orthodox priests, and some young men also have them. No member of the Politburo is bearded. —Reuters

GUESTS at the Midtown Hotel in Boston, Massachusetts, may be startled to find a small cardboard notice under their beds which says: "Hi—we have already looked under the bed to make certain it is clean and sanitary. Thank you."

—"Peterborough" in *The Daily Telegraph*

We pay £25 or more for short items for "Ways of the World." See page 1.

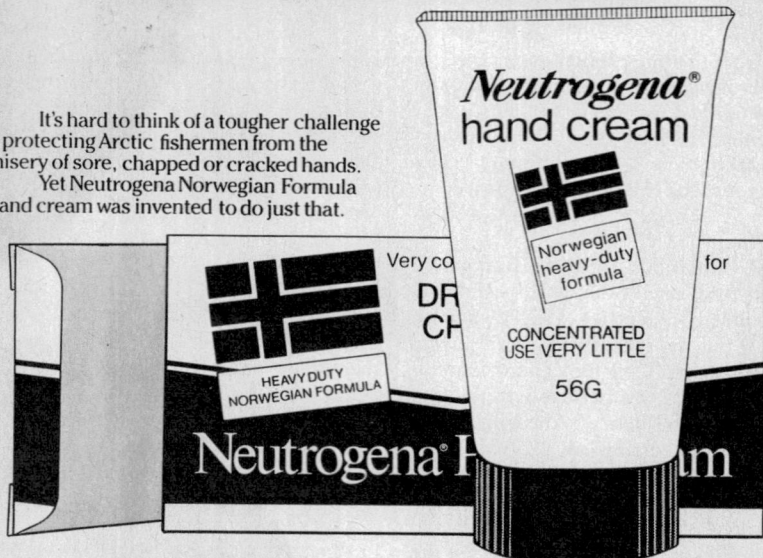

Reader's Digest

ARTICLES OF ENDURING VALUE AND INTEREST

NUCLEAR POWER
Facts and Fears

BY PROFESSOR SIR FRED HOYLE

A leading science thinker reviews the current debate

TEN months ago a nuclear reactor went out of control at the Chernobyl electricity generating station 420 miles from Moscow. The building's roof was blown off in an explosion that has led to the deaths so far of 31 people and the hospitalization of 500 more. A further 135,000 potential victims had to be evacuated from the area.

As the radioactive fall-out spread across Europe, the risk of contamination caused the sale of milk and leaf vegetables to be banned in many parts of eastern Europe, Austria, Italy. In northern Scandinavia, Lapps could no longer eat the reindeer meat and berries that were their staple diet. In Britain,

Safety risk? Britain's controversial Sellafield plant

27

Welsh, Scottish and Cumbrian sheep farmers suffered millions of pounds of losses because of restrictions on the movement and slaughter of contaminated lambs.

Not least of the consequences was the damage to world confidence in the safety of nuclear power.

Here at home, where 38 reactors provide 20 per cent of our electricity, not only politicians but millions of thoughtful, rational people began to question the whole basis of our national energy policy. Is the nuclear risk truly unacceptable, and if so, what are the alternatives? Could we survive without nuclear power?

Running Out. While Britain is particularly blessed with sources of energy, the fact is that stocks will not last indefinitely. According to current geological theory, oil and gas will largely have gone by the middle of the next century. Some believe that our coal might last another 300 years, but only at our current rate of consumption and at a growing cost, not only of money.

This was well expressed by the young doctor in the industry who told me of his own bewilderment that attention appears to be focused on the downside of nuclear power. With passion, he declared, "Just look at what the burning of fossil fuels has done for Britain and the world in terms of mining disasters, of a miners' death-rate from respiratory diseases 40 per cent above the average, of acid rain and pollution of water supplies from abandoned mines."

Certainly part of the price of coal is the thousands more miners who will have their bodies broken underground, while coal fumes do more and more harm to our environment.

Are there no ways of making up the energy shortfall? Could we not harness the energy of the sun, winds, tides? Since 1979, the British Government has invested more than £80 million in research into such possibilities. Sadly, in most cases the capital cost of the technology far outweighs the value of the generated energy, and many of the proposed schemes could damage the environment.

As a keen walker in the Scottish Highlands, I am only too aware of how hydro-electric dams have flooded for ever beautiful lochside paths. And with the constantly varying water levels, no vegetation or wildlife can establish itself at the water's edge. Yet the total hydropower from these desecrated valleys only just exceeds the output from a single nuclear station.

Some theorists have advocated harnessing tidal energy with a barrage in the Severn estuary. But apart from its effects on land drainage, sea defences, water quality and wildlife, the maximum power it could produce would be about five per cent of our *current* electricity demand.

How about wind power? Living in a windy valley 1,400 feet above sea-level, I must be one of the few who could hope to satisfy their electricity needs with a small, short-bladed windmill. But for the nation at large, the prospects are less rosy. For as windmills are made bigger, they become as noisy as helicopters. To come anywhere near meeting Britain's future energy demands, I calculate that we would need 100,000 windmills, spaced half a mile apart over some 23,000 square miles.

In parts of the world where, unlike Britain, sunshine is guaranteed, solar energy has shown its worth in such specific tasks as heating domestic hot water. But the cost of mirrors for tracking the sun and the semiconductors for converting sunlight into electricity has proved too great for large-scale power generation.

Other schemes rest on the possibility of harnessing energy from waves, tapping geothermal heat in the bowels of the earth, fermenting gas from pig slurry, sewage-fed water hyacinths and other vegetation. Yet when all these bits and pieces of alternative energy are added up, even the most optimistic estimates see them as meeting no more than a fraction of our needs. So perhaps we are back to where the problem became acute—at Chernobyl.

For a generation that has grown up in the shadow of the atom bomb, it is understandable that the word nuclear is emotive. Yet a nuclear power-station cannot suffer an *atomic* explosion, as the only way to produce one is with a concentration of fuel and force irrelevant to a nuclear reactor, which merely develops heat to make steam that drives the turbines.

When disaster has struck—as with

Professor Sir Fred Hoyle, 71, is a staff member at the Mount Wilson and Palomar Observatories in California. Formerly Plumian Professor of Astronomy and Experimental Philosophy at Cambridge, he is the author of 47 books on science and outer space. He and his wife live in the Lake District

the explosion at Chernobyl, and the less serious 1979 accident at Three Mile Island power-station in the US—the causes have been human and mechanical error.

In the aftermath of Chernobyl, many have wondered whether such an accident could happen in Britain. The answer is an almost categorical "no." Reactors of the Chernobyl type would not have been approved in any Western country.

In the West, today's reactors sit inside airtight, reinforced-concrete containment buildings designed to keep in radiation and withstand the effects of a plane crash, terrorist bombing or earthquake. Nor does any Western plant operate with the volatile combination of nuclear materials used by the Russians.

There is a Nuclear Installations

Inspectorate in Britain, an independent watch-dog with power to shut down any plant that fails to meet stringent safety standards. Safety-regulated engineering accounts for nearly half the cost of a British nuclear plant.

Good Record. As a result of these provisions, nuclear-industry workers are exposed on average to less than one-tenth of the radiation safety limits set by the International Commission on Radiological Protection. During the 30 years' operation of British nuclear plants, there have been no deaths as a direct result of radiation. And in fewer than 20 cases has it been agreed that radiation might have been a contributory factor in deaths of former employees.

Even so, no one can claim that Britain's nuclear power industry has been without its accidents. In 1957, a fire in a reactor at Sellafield (then known as Windscale) released enough radioactivity for the government to order the destruction of two million litres of local milk.

Following a series of subsequent leaks from the reprocessing plant, the Nuclear Installations Inspectorate published a report highly critical of Sellafield management, which was then drastically restructured. In consequence, Sellafield has suffered its share of damaging headlines—and continues to do so. Last December, following a series of minor incidents earlier in the year, a safety audit by the Inspectorate led to the plant being ordered to begin improving its reprocessing operations within 12 months or face closure.

In its defence, the nuclear industry points out that such an order shows the efficacy of safety regulations, and that in not one of the plant's incidents has the release of radioactivity endangered life. Following its November 1983 spillage into the Irish Sea, it was calculated that a swimmer would have had to hold a piece of contaminated seaweed against the skin for five hours before exceeding the radioactive dosage considered safe in an average year.

Labour MP Norman Atkinson performed a public service last summer when he pointed to a tendency to exaggerate the size and consequences of any nuclear accident. "One recent headlined spillage at Sellafield was safely cleared up with a mop."

The other area of major concern in Britain is the disposal of nuclear waste, the residue of the fission process that remains radioactive. The most highly radioactive waste is kept at Sellafield in double-walled stainless-steel tanks, encased in several feet of concrete, from which there has never been a leak. Less radioactive low-level waste—much of it from hospitals, factories and research institutes—is packed in containers and dumped in deep clay trenches.

The disposal of intermediate-level waste is still under debate; meanwhile, it is being stored on site. UK NIREX (Nuclear Industry Radioactive Waste Executive), the government agency which will be responsible for its disposal, is searching for another low-level disposal site in a clay belt at one of four possible places in Humberside, Lincolnshire, Bedfordshire and Essex.

Reasonably enough, local residents have not welcomed the prospect of living near the chosen site. Even so, with the waste in steel drums inside concrete casks, in a concrete-lined trench and covered with up to 40 feet of clay, those living an entire lifetime near the site would receive no more radioactivity than from a fortnight's holiday in the granite hills of Cornwall.

However reassuring the scientific facts, they still have to assuage a mass of understandable public hostility. How is the nuclear industry to gain the trust of the general public?

Since human error played a large part in the accident at Chernobyl, two obvious courses are improved training and a determination to develop reactors that are "inherently safe" —ones that *cannot* go out of control.

"Inherent safety," *The Economist* recently declared, "means replacing Murphy's law with the law of physics." In one new Swedish design, for example, the reactor core and cooling system are immersed in a solution of water and boron—a liquid capable of damping down the heat-generating chain reaction. If the reactor's cooling system should fail, the borated water floods in to shut the reactor down automatically.

There are other potentially blunder-proof designs, but Britain can contribute to their development only by itself remaining a nuclear power. Furthermore, it is only by continuing our own nuclear role that we can effectively press for higher safety standards abroad. For as a report by the House of Lords Select Committee on the European Communities succinctly put it last August, "A clear lesson of Chernobyl is that immunity from radioactive fall-out cannot be achieved by renouncing nuclear power-stations on one's own national territory. Reactor safety is an international problem."

Whatever Britain does, nuclear power is in the world to stay. Neither the Americans nor the Russians— nor, indeed, many of our European neighbours—are going to rely on dwindling supplies of coal and oil in the certain knowledge that the lights will eventually go out. Britain's obligation does not lie in opting out of the dilemma, but in applying our world-renowned scientific creativity and our moral integrity to the development and operation of *safe* nuclear reactors.

PHOTOGRAPHS: PAGE 27, © BRITISH NUCLEAR FUELS PLC; PAGE 23, CAMERA PRESS

Ear of the Beholder

A MUSIC lover is one who, when told that Raquel Welch sings in the bath, puts his ear to the keyhole.
—Lord Constantine of Stanmore,
quoted by Jack Aspinwall in *Hit Me Again!* (Buchan & Enright)

With Dudley Moore in "10"

"The Sound of Music"

"Victor/Victoria"

STARRING Julie Andrews

BY PAULA DRANOV

There's much more to this multi-talented actress than a sweet voice and a pretty face

"Duet for One"

IT'S picture-postcard perfect and a group of tourists are drinking it all in: blue sky, the snow-capped Swiss Alps towering majestically over green fields dotted with wild flowers. Then comes that familiar line, "The hills are alive with the sound of music," and suddenly, into view runs . . . could it be?

"I know they recognized me," Julie Andrews says with a laugh. "They must think I do that all the time. Maria von Trapp for ever!"

It's a story that Miss Andrews loves to tell against herself. At the time, she was at her home in Gstaad, working to get in shape physically and vocally for a London concert. "I was doing a lot of running up and down hills," she explains, "and from time to time I would test my voice."

For millions around the world, Julie Andrews will always be Baroness Maria, whom she portrayed in the 1965 film *The Sound of Music*. Curiously, her own life resembles her film heroine's, filled with children and song, and even mountains, at least when she's in Switzerland.

"Julie Andrews transcends the screen, almost reaching out and hugging the audience," a critic wrote. Audiences return the hug. Despite an erratic career—she's had her share of box-office flops and made no films at all in the mid-1970s—she is one of Hollywood's most enduringly popular stars.

She seems to have aged not at all in the 20 years since *The Sound of Music*. Her trade-mark cap of red-gold hair has been slightly modified and is now more elegant than elfin. She is athletically slim, and her creamy complexion glows with health and energy.

Julie's roles have ranged from the cockney flower girl, Eliza Doolittle, in the hit musical *My Fair Lady*, to the down-and-out singer pretending to be a man pretending to be a woman in the

film comedy *Victor/Victoria*. But the real Julie Andrews is more like . . . well, Maria von Trapp. She is a homebody ambivalent about her career. She loves to act and sing, but regularly turns down work that would take her away from her family. "If you're happily married and love what you're doing," she says, "it seems dumb to go off to Siberia for five months to shoot a film."

Julie Andrews was born in 1935 in Walton-on-Thames, Surrey. Her father was a teacher, her mother a pianist. When she was four, her parents divorced and her mother married Ted Andrews, a Canadian tenor. It was he who discovered that little Julie had a big, big voice with an amazing five-octave range.

Early Promise. Julie was ten when she joined her parents' music-hall act. She had to stand on a box to reach the microphone, but she was an immediate success. The Andrewses toured Britain playing theatres a week at a time, moving from one seedy boarding-house to another.

In ankle socks, strap shoes and dresses cut to flatten her bosom, Julie performed as a child well into her teens. When her voice matured, her range dropped to three octaves and she was convinced her career was over. But in 1953 the director of a forthcoming New York production of *The Boy Friend* saw her in a panto-mime at the London Hippodrome, and offered her a role. *The Boy Friend* made her a star at 19. A year later she got the part of Eliza Doolittle in a musical version of Shaw's *Pygmalion*. *My Fair Lady* was a sensation. After two years on Broadway, Julie played Eliza in London for 18 months. Then she returned to the New York stage as Guinevere opposite Richard Burton's King Arthur in *Camelot*.

Yet the young actress wasn't considered a big enough box-office draw in Hollywood. Rex Harrison was asked to repeat his Henry Higgins role in the film version of *My Fair Lady*, but producer Jack Warner cast Audrey Hepburn as Eliza. Julie was still smarting when Walt Disney asked her to play in a film musical *he* had in mind: *Mary Poppins*.

In 1964, accepting the Golden Globe best-actress award for her performance as the eccentric nanny—she would also win that year's Oscar—Julie purred into the microphone: "I would also like to thank Jack Warner for making this possible." There was silence in the hall, for the powerful Warner was in the front row. Then the crowd—including Warner—roared with appreciative laughter.

Variety Acts. Julie Andrews is more than a sweet voice and pretty face, but it took nearly 20 years for Hollywood to accept that fact. True, she was a star during the mid-1960s. Her second film, *The Americanization of Emily*, was praised by the critics, and her third, *The Sound of Music*, was a block-buster. Still, to escape type-casting, Julie gambled on unsympathetic roles—playing the temperamental actress Gertrude Lawrence in *Star!*, an enemy spy in *Darling Lili*, and a traitorous secretary in *The Tamarind Seed*. All were critical and financial disasters.

In 1969 she married Blake Edwards, a screen-writer, director and producer. Julie had a seven-year-old daughter, Emma Kate, born of an earlier marriage to British set designer Tony Walton. Edwards had a daughter, Jennifer, 11, and a son, Geoff, aged nine.

Julie made what she calls a "very conscious decision" to put her family first, at the expense of her career if need be. She stayed at home with the children until she started work on a 1972 American television series, "The Julie Andrews Hour." That same year, Blake decided to concentrate on his writing. He worked at home and took care of the children while Julie focused on the show.

The role reversal was not wholly successful. "I love being a mother and a wife *and* an actress," Julie says, "but I was not comfortable with just going to work and having everything else taken care of." Julie was back to her favourite roles—wife and mother—when the family moved to Switzerland a year later.

In 1974, disappointed that they hadn't had a child together, Julie and Blake decided to adopt, applying to an agency that was placing Vietnamese war orphans. Within a year, five-month-old Amy arrived, followed by two-month-old Joanna.

"Both girls were exceedingly small and malnourished when they arrived," Julie recalls. "They had scabies, a contagious skin infection, and one also had bronchitis. But it was incredible to see how they blossomed in just a few weeks. It was like watering a flower."

Julie is determined that her children have a normal childhood despite their parents' celebrity. "She always tries to be a mum first," says Emma, now at 24 an aspiring actress. "Even when she is busiest, she makes time for the family. She's always there to read a bedtime story or to go for a quiet walk and talk in the garden. Inevitably she is the one to clean up after a family pet. She will look up and sigh, 'I wonder if Elizabeth Taylor does this.'"

New Role. In 1979 Julie and Blake heard of an airlift organized by Los Angeles lawyers Richard Walden and Llewellyn Werner to rush food and medical supplies to Malaysia for Vietnamese boat people.

"Blake and Julie gave us 10,000 dollars," says Walden. A few weeks later, they donated 75,000 dollars to charter a plane taking medical supplies to Cambodia. Then the couple set about attracting Hollywood's big names—and big money—to charity events for the organization, now known as Operation California.

The relief agency has since distributed 37 million dollars in aid to El Salvador, Nicaragua, Lebanon, Poland, Ethiopia and Somalia as well as Vietnam and Cambodia. "It's impossible to quantify in monetary terms the support they've given us," says Walden. "Without them, we would have ceased to exist."

In 1982 Julie decided to see at first-hand the conditions in orphanages and camps in Vietnam, Cambodia and Thailand. "I will remember this place to my dying day," she wrote after visiting an orphanage. "It was run down, with nothing to stimulate the children—no colour, no posters, no toys.

"We went into the really-diseased-kids' area, and I couldn't believe my eyes. The children were in cots with wooden slats, no mattresses. The stench of urine was appalling. One room with just babies. Some had encephalitis, some polio, some were blind, one with a terrible cleft palate, some were dying of malnutrition." Julie returned home determined to devote even more time to relief work.

Her tireless efforts attracted attention. In 1983, President Reagan presented Operation California with the President's Volunteer Action Award. And in June 1984, Julie was invited by the United Nations High Commissioner for Refugees to a conference on African relief.

Meanwhile, Julie's professional career took on new momentum. Her husband lured her back to the screen after four years absence to play the "older woman" in *10*. Next she portrayed a movie queen with a too-good-to-be-true public image—not unlike her own—in *S.O.B*.

The 1982 production *Victor/Victoria* scored her a personal triumph. In a single climactic scene she superimposed a vivid new image over the ghost of Maria von Trapp. Clad in sequins, she slithered sensuously through a song-and-dance number. Then, after acknowledging the tumultuous applause, she tore off her wig, revealing that "she" was a "he."

It was an unforgettable moment.

In *Duet for One*, opening in Britain this month, Julie tackles another taxing role: that of a concert violinist struck down by multiple sclerosis. It is one she approached with characteristic thoroughness, taking violin lessons to give authenticity to her screen "performances."

On stage or off, Julie Andrews has never been afraid of hard work. The late Moss Hart, who directed her 30 years ago in *My Fair Lady*, paid affectionate tribute to his tenacious young star: "Julie can rise to any occasion." She can and she does—with grace, elegance and her own special warmth and generosity.

PHOTOGRAPHS: KOBAL COLLECTION; NATIONAL FILM ARCHIVE; © 1986 CANNON FILMS, INC.
ILLUSTRATION: NEIL MACDONALD

Taxi!

HAVING asked the receptionist at the Rossyia Hotel in Moscow where the nearest night-club was, a US official was told: "In Helsinki, sir."

—Leopold Unger in *International Herald Tribune*

The Sacrificial Tree

BY EWAN CLARKSON

**My one-man conservation effort got off to
a flourishing start...**

WHEN I was 37 I came to live in the small
thatched cottage where my father had spent the
last few years of his life. The cottage was old,
and over the centuries it seemed to have settled com-
placently into the fat, fertile land of the Devon valley.

Apple trees raised crabbed arthritic fingers to shelter it

from the prevailing winds. A long, lean rasher of a garden stretched for a hundred yards alongside the lane.

At the end of the garden and across the lane lay the spinney, a ragged remnant of forgotten wilderness. Few people ventured past the barrier of thorns that guarded the overgrown gate. The path, such as it was, led nowhere, trodden only by the feet of badgers, foxes, rabbits, and my own.

It was in the winter that I first noticed the weeping birch. It stood in a far corner, a little apart from the oaks and the ash, the elms and the hazel. The morning had been grey with mist and heavy dew, and now a stray sunbeam pierced the cloud, highlighting the tree so that each drooping twig shone with a thousand glimmering diamond drops.

At that moment I fell in love with the tree. I even came to think of it as she—an anthropomorphism which I felt was a harmless weakness—for the tree had a feminine grace in all seasons. Young green of April after a passing shower. Cascade of autumn gold. Lace-work of twigs black against a rising winter moon.

The years passed and the weeping birch grew taller. Then came news that a highway was to be built, right through the spinney. Ironically, I was to become materially richer. I would lose my tumbledown old garage, and

CUMBERLAND-BORN writer Ewan Clarkson, aged 58, lives near Newton Abbot with his wife Jenny. Specializing in nature topics, he is a regular newspaper columnist and author of eight novels, most recent of which are *The Wake of the Storm* and *Ice Trek* (Century).

the end of my garden. In return I would get a new garage, and the lane would become mine, more than doubling the size of my garden. What, though, would be the fate of the weeping birch?

From the plans of the proposed development I discovered to my relief that with a little care the birch could be preserved. It was close to the highway, to be sure, but not so near that it could not be avoided, so long as all concerned were aware of its existence.

The day the woodcutters arrived to start the preliminary clearing, I went up and spoke to them. Tree-lovers all they turned out to be, and each agreed that there was no reason to take down the weeping birch. Privately, perhaps, they reasoned that should the need arise, one shove from a bulldozer would shoulder the tree out of the way, but since its wood was of no value to them, they could afford to ignore it.

Privately I too feared for the future safety of the tree, so when the construction gang arrived I lined them all up, surveyors, planners, contractors, the works foreman, and introduced them to my tree. I even resorted to a small subterfuge: I told the men that the tree was especially beloved by the women of the village, and that I shuddered to think of their fate should they molest it.

Something worked. Throughout the summer, as clouds of dust filled the air and the roar of earth-moving machinery echoed from morning to night, the tree stood unscathed.

There came a day when the low hum of traffic replaced the cacophony of construction. I had a new garage, and a new garden to till. A high mound separated me from the road, but above it the weeping birch, now 30 years old and as many feet tall, towered in graceful splendour against the sky. I felt I could relax.

Next spring came unseasonably hot and dry, baking the earth of my new-laid garden to the consistency of cement. One morning I was outside, struggling to break up the recalcitrant clods, when I heard the dreaded sound of an earth-moving machine.

I raced to the top of the mound. A bulldozer was heading straight towards my tree. I rushed across, waving my arms and shouting until I had the attention of the operator.

A benign-looking lad with thick spectacles, he peered at the tree as though it was the first time he had noticed it, and cheerfully nodded his assent. Sure he could miss the birch. He was merely taking out a trench for an electricity cable, and he could easily go round it.

Now I felt easier in my mind than ever before, for surely no one would go poking round with a bulldozer where a high-voltage cable was laid. My tree was safer than if it were surrounded by a high security fence.

Summer passed, and slowly the landscape began to mellow as the scars of intervention healed. With the autumn the barometer fell. Dark clouds began to gather, building brooding ramparts above the hunched shoulder of Dartmoor. That night the wind freshened, driving the clouds before it, flinging great gusts of rain on to the parched earth, filling the gutters and flooding the blocked, neglected drains.

Morning dawned fresh and clear, with fluffy white clouds racing by to put a final polish on the washed-out blue of the sky. A quick check round the garden revealed little amiss. The storm, it appeared, had passed without leaving too much havoc.

It was then that I saw the birch, or rather what was left of her. Twenty feet above the ground the trunk ended in a ragged, weeping stump. Her crown had gone, torn to the ground by the wind. She had lost her grace and beauty for ever.

If the experience has taught me anything, it is that the Creator prefers this planet in an advanced state of dilapidation and decay. For a while, though, I couldn't help wishing that when He was moving in His mysterious ways, He would watch where He was putting His big feet.

ILLUSTRATION: PETER BARRETT

Facial Discrimination

ACTOR Paul Newman: "I have often thought that my tombstone might well read: 'Here lies Paul Newman, who died a failure because his eyes suddenly turned brown...' "

Rescue from a Blazing Tanker

BY JOHN BEATTIE

In the teeth of a blizzard, an Air Force hero began a desperate mission

LIGHT-HEADED from the fumes he had inhaled during his descent through clouds of blinding black smoke, RAF helicopter winchman Melvyn Ward reeled along the pitching deck of the Greek oil tanker *Orleans* as she wallowed out of control in the North Sea, 65 miles north-east of Great Yarmouth.

A blizzard was raging, its howl backgrounding the cacophony of shouts from the crew, the clop-clop of the Sea King rescue helicopter above and the relentless shriek of the ship's siren. Through his boot soles Ward could feel the heat from the inferno that was raging deep inside the ship. Columns of flame shot into the air from oil blazing on the sea's surface.

The 155,000-ton tanker, en route from Shetland to Southampton Water, had been damaged in a collision with a Dutch fishing boat. Her hull was sliced open, and within seconds her cargo of crude oil was ablaze. Now 60 mph gales were driving the crippled ship inexorably towards the gas platforms of the Sean fields. Mel Ward tried not to think about the nightmare consequences if she bore down on one of the rigs. He had a more immediate problem: to rescue the 32 souls on board.

Less than an hour earlier, at 7.23am on January 24, 1986, Ward had been shaken awake in the dispersal hut where he was on stand-by at RAF Coltishall, a fighter station near Norwich. Clambering into his flying kit, the 41-year-old Master Air

Loadmaster joined his colleagues on the duty search and rescue crew—Master Air Electronics Operator John Reeson and co-pilot Flight Lieutenant Martin Powell.

The men received a quick briefing by the captain, Flight Lieutenant Charles Gillow. Then the four of them were airborne, heading northeast into buffeting wind and swirling snow on board the yellow Sea King of "C" Flight, 202 Squadron—call sign "Rescue 25."

At 8.05am the helicopter nosed gingerly into the smoke billowing from the stricken ship. Balls of blazing, superheated oil whooshed menacingly past as Ward checked his lifejacket and shrugged into the winch harness to spin down on the wire into impenetrable blackness.

Swinging violently over the tanker's starboard afterdeck, he landed sprawling with a force that winded him. Quickly he freed himself from the harness, but kept tight hold of the 150-foot highline, a light rope tied to the bottom of the winch wire so he could haul the canvas lifting loops—the strops—within reach when needed.

Take Over. Pandemonium raged among the terrified seamen as Ward shoved them into some semblance of order. At last, a ragged queue snaked along the heaving deck and Ward pulled down the strops. The sailors surged forward.

"Two!" shouted Ward, handing them off. *"Deux! Dos!"* He bundled the first pair towards the stern rail,

guided them into the strops and gave a thumbs-up signal to John Reeson in the Sea King 100 feet above.

The pair were whisked off their feet and swallowed up in a billow of smoke. Minutes later, Ward again hauled in the strops. Two more—one of them an officer's wife—were jerked aloft. Then everything, in Ward's words, "turned into a can of worms" as the blizzard suddenly redoubled its fury. Huge gushes of smoke mushroomed upwards, engulfing the helicopter and blinding the pilots. In imminent peril of crashing the Sea King into the ship, they backed off.

Now or Never. As the highline slithered out of Ward's gloved grip and the clatter of the Sea King faded, he heard an ominous new sound—a thundering rumble from deep inside *Orleans*. Tons more oil had reached flashpoint and exploded. Already a barrier of smoke and flames had risen between the afterdeck and the lifeboats.

Elbowing through the cluster of seamen round him, Ward grabbed the skipper, Dimitrios Kyriazis: "Captain, we can't winch from the deck, and we can't reach the lifeboats. We must launch an inflatable dinghy."

He turned to supervise the launching. The dinghy hit the water and inflated upside-down. Ward swore; righting it would be one more drain on his dwindling strength.

He turned back to the captain. "I'll jump in the sea and your crew must follow, two at a time. When everyone is in the dinghy and away from the smoke, the helicopter can lift us all clear."

The skipper glanced in disbelief at the upturned raft tossing in seething seas 80 feet below. "But..." he began.

"It's the only way, sir," Ward said curtly.

He clambered over the ship's rail and turned, elbow crooked around a stanchion. His stomach churned as he looked down the ship's flank, falling away like the wall of a high-rise office-block. He knew that unless he jumped then, he would never jump at all. Gulping a huge lungful of air, he let go.

"Somehow I managed to jump at the moment when the sea was furthest away," he says. He remembers only a terrific bang as he smacked into the water at almost 50 mph. His next recollection is of struggling to right the upturned dinghy.

As he scrabbled for a grip, *Orleans* rolled and her stern slammed down, launching a huge wave towards the winchman. Ward found himself cartwheeling through the air, ten feet above the waves, while the dinghy took off in the opposite direction like a child's runaway hoop.

In Peril. Choking and retching, Ward tried swimming, but felt himself being dragged back towards the *Orleans*, until the steel cliff of the ship's side was right over him. Helpless, he was sucked beneath the hull.

For a moment his mind was a jumble of thoughts—his childhood in Nottinghamshire, his present home in a Norfolk village, his wife Val and their daughters Christine, 18, and Karen, 15. Would he see them again?

A terrible pounding filled his ears, and he watched in horror as a huge propeller rotated towards him. Somehow he escaped from the vortex, rolling over and over towards the great steel rudder. "I remember thinking: 'My God, that's the size of my house!' and then the stern sank into a trough. I saw it coming down towards me and began to swim for my life. When I next looked I was 30 yards away. The crew of the chopper had me in sight and lowered a strop to me."

But Ward didn't call a halt. Back on board the Sea King, he could see that a patch of the tanker's afterdeck was now clear of smoke. He resolved to go down again, this time using two highlines tied together to give him a 300-foot link with the winch wire, enabling the pilot to hover further from the smoke and flames.

He was weary, sick from the oil and sea-water he had swallowed, when he crashed on deck for the second time. He drove back the seamen who fought to get to the strops, helped the first two into the loops and signalled to Reeson. Then disaster struck.

As the pair lifted off the deck, *Orleans* rolled violently and the winch wire twisted round two navigation lights fitted to a flagstaff above the stern rail. Unable to see what was happening, Reeson kept feeding power to the winch motor.

With a loud crack the wire, breaking strain 3,700 pounds, snapped. Fortunately for the two men in the strops, one end spiralled round the flagstaff and held them dangling outboard of the rail. The other section scythed upwards and wrapped itself round the rotor head in the centre of the chopper's five spinning blades.

Desperately, pilot Charles Gillow wrenched at the controls as the Sea King began to lose height. For what seemed unending seconds the terror went on. Then, with a surge of hope, the 28-year-old captain felt the controls begin to respond. The damaged rotor had flung out the winch wire and was once again clawing evenly at the air. But surely the helicopter was too crippled to land? "I ordered the crew to prepare for ditching," Gillow recalls.

A scant 30 feet above the sea, he changed his mind. On the radar screen Reeson had located a drilling-rig helipad some nine miles away. Gillow decided there was a chance they could make it. The helicopter started to creep forwards.

Ward knew none of this. He had watched numbly as Rescue 25 dipped and disappeared in the rolling banks of smoke.

Screams of fear alerted him to the two Greeks still swinging like marionettes from the flagstaff. Ignoring the dizzy drop over the stern, he

Master Air Loadmaster Melvyn Ward

climbed over the rails and shinned up the staff. Supported by three of the *Orleans* crew, he unravelled the wire and helped the men back to the safety of the afterdeck.

That safety, he knew, was illusory. Although the smoke and flame had cleared sufficiently to allow access to a lifeboat, renewed explosions were ripping through the oil in the tanks; the ship, still out of control, remained on course for the gas platforms.

Once more Ward sought out Captain Kyriazis. "The helicopter has gone," he shouted. "We must abandon ship, Captain."

The Captain nodded gravely. "The lifeboat on the port side will take you all," he said. "I will stay on board with four of my men. Maybe there is something we can do. Good luck . . . and thank you."

The slow descent in the lifeboat was almost as traumatic as Ward's earlier, more abrupt entry into the sea. The fibreglass boat swung uncontrollably, crashing against the ship's side so hard that it threatened to pitch them all into the water.

Ward ordered everyone to use the oars as fenders. As the seamen put down their bundles of possessions to grab the oars, an astonished Ward found himself staring at a canary in a cage. With a feeling of unreality he added it to his mental tally of those rescued.

At that instant they hit the ship's side with such force that every oar splintered, sending lethal shards of wood flying. Then they were down, roller-coasting on a white-capped crest towards the tanker's stern. All around patches of sea were on fire as oil continued to pour from the ruptured hull.

But help was at hand. Instructed by HM Coastguard, the gas platform stand-by vessel *Boston Sea Stallion* had been waiting near by throughout the drama. As soon as the lifeboat was clear of the tanker, she came battering through the mountainous seas to pick them up.

As the two boats see-sawed on the waves, the seamen started pulling themselves up the scrambling nets on *Boston Sea Stallion*. Bemusedly, Ward watched the caged canary being hauled to safety before reaching for the net himself.

On board, great news awaited: Rescue 25 had managed to put down on the helipad of the Charles Rowan drilling rig. She was badly damaged but her crew were unhurt.

His spirits lifted by the news, Ward grinned wearily at the *Boston Sea Stallion*'s mate. "I'd like to go below now," he said.

Captain Kyriazis was rescued later that day, when the fire died down sufficiently for a tug to get lines on board *Orleans* and tow her to Rotterdam. And on July 22, 1986, watched by his proud wife and daughters, Master Air Loadmaster Melvyn Ward stood to attention at Buckingham Palace while the Queen pinned to his chest the Air Force Cross, one of the service's highest awards for bravery.

ILLUSTRATION: MICHAEL TURNER

Time Traveller

DURING a weekend visit to an unfamiliar city, my elderly father became aware of just how much times have changed. When car trouble developed, he left my mother in the hotel and ventured out into heavy traffic in search of a garage. To his immense relief, just a few hundred yards from the hotel, he saw a large sign: THE BODY SHOP—GET YOUR BATTERY CHARGED.

My father parked the car, hurried inside and found—to his astonishment —that he had just entered his first topless bar.   —J. Watson

Three years ago, when Reader's Digest published its first article about AIDS, Britain had suffered 18 victims with six deaths. Since then some 600 cases have been recorded in this country, with around 300 deaths. A further 30,000–40,000 men, women and children are now believed to be carrying the AIDS virus. These figures double every ten months, and today doctors speak of AIDS as Britain's—and the world's—most alarming scourge.

One of this country's leading experts on AIDS is Dr Anthony Pinching, 39, senior lecturer and consultant in Immunology at St Mary's Hospital Medical School, London, who has treated more than 130 AIDS patients. Here he provides forthright answers to questions about the disease.

'Dr Pinching, What Are My Chances of Getting AIDS?'

THIS depends almost entirely on you and the behaviour of your sexual partner. For a couple in a faithful, monogamous relationship, the risk of developing AIDS is almost nil. The more sexual partners someone has, the greater their chances of contracting the AIDS virus—though just one unlucky or unwise encounter can be infectious.

So far some 90 per cent of AIDS victims in the United Kingdom have been male homosexuals, who tend to have more sexual partners than heterosexuals. Another high-risk group is intravenous drug users who share needles.

But we now know the infection can spread in the general community—from men to women, and from women back to men, though probably not quite as easily, as the virus is more concentrated in semen than in vaginal secretions. In some African countries, AIDS occurs among men and women almost equally.

The real danger is thus not so much homosexuality as having more than one partner. "Casual sex," notes one concerned observer, has become "a bit like Russian roulette—in sleeping with one partner, you are effectively sleeping with all of that person's previous partners."

What is AIDS?

Acquired Immune Deficiency Syndrome is a sexually transmitted disease caused by a virus that so weakens part of the body's natural immune system that it cannot fight off certain infections from other sources. Since the Human Immunodeficiency Virus (HIV) works in a highly selective way, AIDS victims can withstand many common infections such as flu. But they are vulnerable to illnesses that would not normally affect them, yet whose germs are latent in many of us: pneumonia, diarrhoea, brain infections.

The commonest early infection is a rare chest disease: *pneumocystis carinii pneumonia*. The AIDS virus can also lead to a skin disease—*Kaposi's sarcoma*—that causes purplish tumours almost anywhere on the body, and to a brain infection that causes dementia.

First sign of trouble is the appearance of antibodies to the AIDS virus in the bloodstream, usually one to three months after infection. All those identified as "antibody-positive" will, however well they look and feel, carry and be able to transmit the virus for the rest of their lives.

Within three years of infection, around one in five will develop full-scale AIDS and die—usually within another three years. But with the illness still in its infancy, our knowledge of it remains incomplete, and the proportion of carriers who develop AIDS could eventually turn out to be higher.

How is the AIDS virus passed on?

The virus can be transmitted in only three ways: from infected semen or vaginal secretions in sexual intercourse—either vaginal or anal; from blood-to-blood contact and from an infected mother to her unborn child. Shared drug needles and syringes are the main way that the virus spreads from blood to blood.

Can you have sex without risking infection?

To be absolutely safe, have a single sexual partner who is faithful and not already a carrier. Otherwise, both heterosexuals and homosexuals should reduce the number of their sexual partners, avoid anal *and* vaginal penetration or, if having intercouse, use a sheath. Also risky, though possibly less so, is oral sex.

Is AIDS infectious like flu or measles?

No. The virus is probably one of the most fragile and least infectious ever identified because it doesn't survive long outside the body. Unlike colds, flu or measles the AIDS virus cannot be spread by sneezing, sharing utensils or by being near an infected person. There is no known instance of the virus having been transmitted from cups, towels, lavatories, telephones, drinking fountains, whirlpool baths, library books.

Can the virus be passed on through saliva?

There is no recorded case of this happening. Although the virus is known to exist in saliva and tears, it does so either in a form unable to transmit the disease or in concentrations far too minute. Worries about dental instruments or the Communion chalice in church are unfounded. Natural caution, however, would suggest avoiding "deep kissing"— French kissing—with someone you don't know well.

Can you catch the virus from giving the kiss of life?

No, not unless the person receiving aid is bleeding heavily from the mouth. Even in that case the risk is slight, but the person giving aid should avoid as much blood as possible. Wipe it away, form a barrier with a handkerchief or piece of cloth, and wash immediately afterwards.

Could my child be infected from a mass inoculation programme?

Any such programme will employ sterilized or disposable equipment which poses no risk.

Outside this area of disciplined medical practice, though, everyone should be cautious about sharing any device that punctures the skin—hypodermic needles, syringes, ear-piercing equipment, tattooing or acupuncture needles—unless such instruments are disposable or have been sterilized.

Can you catch the virus from a blood transfusion?

The risk of this happening is now infinitesimally small. Before the danger was recognized, some people, particularly haemophiliacs, caught the virus from contaminated blood or blood products. The National Blood Transfusion Service now screens all donated blood. In addition, all blood products needed by haemophiliacs are heat-treated to kill off the AIDS virus. (Whole blood cannot be heat-treated, as this destroys the red cells.)

However, since the tell-tale antibodies to the virus do not appear until some weeks after infection, the total effectiveness of blood screening depends on those in high-risk groups *not* donating blood. To help ensure that they are excluded, all potential donors must sign forms to indicate that they understand why certain groups are asked not to give blood and to show their consent to their own blood being given an AIDS test.

Can a blood donor get the virus?

Absolutely not. If you are donating blood to the National Blood Transfusion Service, new, sterile needles for sampling and taking blood are used for each donor and then discarded.

How do I know if I have the AIDS virus?

If you think you are at risk, a simple blood test can be carried out at any of the STD (Sexually Transmitted Disease) clinics run by hospitals in major cities. This confidential test identifies AIDS virus antibodies in the bloodstream and the result is made known to the patient within a few weeks. Because a positive result can have devastating psychological effects on the victim, careful counselling is given before and after any test.

Some carriers remain perfectly well after infection. Others may develop swollen glands and possibly fever, heavy sweating at night, rapid weight loss, persistent diarrhoea, profound fatigue: symptoms of what is known as AIDS-related complex (ARC). But it is important to remember that most of these symptoms also occur in flu and with many other viral infections. It's only if several such indications occur together, and they persist, that the AIDS virus might be the cause.

Is there any treatment for AIDS?

There is no treatment for the virus or damage to the immune system. But much can be done to alleviate the accompanying infections and tumours and, between these bouts of sickness, the patient can remain perfectly fit and well for months.

There is some evidence that the virus carrier can reduce the chances of the full-scale illness developing by eating a balanced diet, avoiding stress, giving up smoking, drinking only in moderation, getting enough rest and exercise. There is no reason why the virus carrier should not continue with any sport.

Doctors urge sexual responsibility on carriers—not only to avoid the spread of infection, but because it is now known that other sexually transmitted diseases can spark the virus into action and thus increase the risk of AIDS.

Do women face particular problems with AIDS?

Yes. A carrier who becomes pregnant stands a higher chance of developing the illness because pregnancy may increase the activity of the virus and its effect on her immune system.

Still more harrowing is the 50 per cent chance of passing on the virus to the unborn child. One out of two of these infected babies will develop AIDS within two years—and die within another year.

Is death from AIDS certain?

Yes. Virtually all patients with AIDS die within four years.

Is there any chance of a cure, or a vaccine?

Not for the foreseeable future. Worldwide, medical research units and drug companies are working flat out on the problem, but no responsible person is yet talking of a "cure." The most that drugs have been able to do is alleviate some of the AIDS symptoms.

All AIDS anti-viral drugs are still highly experimental, and may prove too toxic for general use. In trials, AZT—azidothymidine—seems to have helped patients gain weight and reduced infections, but can cause severe anaemia. This and other drugs also offer some hope in halting the spread of the virus from cell to cell.

The major problem facing those searching for either cure or vaccine is the variable chemistry of the AIDS virus. As virologist Dr Angus Dalgleish of London's Northwick Park Hospital puts it, "A vaccine works by warning the body's immune system to look out for a certain virus, just as police seek stolen cars by their registration numbers. Unfortunately, the AIDS virus keeps randomly changing its number plates."

How do I behave to an acquaintance or colleague who is a carrier?

You cannot catch the AIDS virus through ordinary work-place or social contact—and by showing that you know such basic facts you can provide some reassurance. Remember that the AIDS victim is likely to suffer feelings of isolation and rejection experienced by victims of few other diseases. More than at any other point in their lives, such people need the support of family, friends and colleagues.

To give such support is, I believe, not only morally right, but crucial to the containment of AIDS. For if we go round blaming and isolating those with the illness, we can hardly expect them to change their behaviour for the benefit of a society that is condemning them.

For further information, contact: Terrence Higgins Trust, BM AIDS, London WC1N 3XX (01-833 2971); Haemophilia Society, 123 Westminster Bridge Road, London SE1 (01-928 2020); Healthline AIDS Information Service (01-980 4848/981 2717); Health Education Council, 78 New Oxford Street, London WC1 (01-637 1881); Scottish AIDS Monitor, PO Box 169, Edinburgh EH3 3UU (031-558 1167).

Petpourri

MY YOUNG son and I spent much time in pet shops looking for just the right fish for his aquarium and for snails to keep the tank clean.

One day he came home from a shopping trip all excited to tell me he had discovered some African frogs that really did a good job cleaning the aquarium.

"Good," I said. "Then you won't have to buy any snails."

"Oh, yes," he said. "I'll have to buy them too. Those frogs don't do windows."
—Mrs R. Raymond

Humour in Uniform

ALL military personnel love status, and display their rank and position on their vehicle identification plates. Those in the Falkland Islands are no exception.

In a car-park in Port Stanley, I noticed the usual group of Land Rovers with their identifying plates: "OC FILOG," "OC CATERING SQN," "CQMS FIPAS," "CDR BFFI." One vehicle, however, had a plate which read: "NOBODY IN PARTICULAR."

—Squadron Leader Warwick Woodhouse, Richmond, North Yorkshire

As a marine on a US Navy ship in the Mediterranean, I went to the barber for the first time, and my attention quickly focused on his unique cutting style. He started at the top of the head and cut down the sides. I asked him where he had learnt to cut hair.

"Well, sir," he responded in a drawl, "when they asked who knew how, I told them I'd never cut hair—but I used to shear sheep." —Major Phillip Hughey

Our eight-month-old daughter, born during the last war, had only ever seen her father in uniform, and usually smoking a pipe. Once, in a crowded train compartment, we sat near two soldiers, both smoking pipes. To the amusement of the other passengers—and to my embarrassment—the infant greeted both soldiers in turn with beaming smiles and ecstatic cries of "Dad-dad-dad-dad!"

Faced with such enthusiasm, the "surrogate fathers" took this mistaken identity in good part. One turned to the other and said, in a tone of resignation: "All right, I'll toss you for it."

—Mrs A. Flynn, Upton, Merseyside

EARLY in my training as a pilot I tried to impress an instructor with my knowledge of aerodynamics. He interrupted me with a seasoned pilot's explanation: "Push forward on the stick, and the houses get bigger. Pull back, and the houses get smaller. Keep pulling back, and the houses get big again."

—Jere Matty

THE day before a big military parade in West Germany, a rehearsal was to be held with a general standing in for the royal visitor. Some young subalterns decided to liven up the proceedings.

As the tanks passed the general, their guns swivelled then dipped sharply in salute—stranding the surprised general in a sea of gently bouncing tennis-balls. —Malcolm Webb, Bracknell, Berkshire

We offer £100 for your "Humour in Uniform" story. Details are on page 1.

Lisbon Story

BY GEORGE KENT

Once upon a time, a city fell in love with the sea. The affair is still alive—and sparkling

SEAWEED *in its hair, seagulls on its shoulders* is how a Portuguese poet describes Lisbon.

You smell the ocean's salt in the winds that blow in the city. You walk on it, for the tile patterns of pavements are waves and knots and coiling lines. You see it reflected in the monuments with their stone ropes and rigging, anchors and coral and sea shells. In June when crowds trundle through the town honouring the feasts of Saint Anthony and Saint Peter, the images of the saints clutch small ships. Lisbon itself has a sea shape: its seven hills roll up into crests like breakers about to burst on a beach.

Portugal, almost 350 miles long, only 90 miles wide in places, is like a barge moored to the mainland of Europe. Lisbon, the capital, is where the river Tagus—deep, tawny, slow-moving, wide as a lake at the capital—flows into the Atlantic. Looking out from the city's hills at the breathtaking waterscapes, you suddenly realize that Lisbon is one of the

The Monument of the Discoveries commemorates Prince Henry the Navigator. Below: one of the ancient, narrow streets

most beautiful harbours on earth. Unlike most other big cities, it is clean, shipshape. A sailor metropolis, it is scrubbed and holystoned, lashed dry by the ocean winds.

It was no accident that the men of this city were once the world's great mariners and discoverers. Who was the first to realize Europe's ancient dream of sailing to India? Vasco da Gama. Who were the earliest Europeans to set foot in Japan, Newfoundland, Brazil, China, Angola, the Azores, Madeira? Portuguese.

Changing Hands. Most of the old sea rovers of history have peered through the porthole that is Lisbon, starting with the Romans. Battle-happy barbarian tribes followed, then the Visigoths, and finally the North African Moors. Each came, saw, conquered and, in turn, was conquered and went away. The Moors left the most enduring impression. You can see it in the people's swarthy features, in the architecture; hear it in the language, in the music.

The grandeur of Lisbon, which was to become one of the richest cities on earth, began in the fourteenth century with King John I. He had, among his many children, four sons with a touch of genius; the greatest of them all, born in 1394, was Prince Henry the Navigator.

Except for two voyages to Morocco, Henry did little navigating. He was great because he convinced others that the world was far larger than Europe and the Mediterranean.

In his castle and observatory he organized scholarly conferences of sea captains, astronomers and geographers where, in time, the art of setting a course by the stars and the sun advanced. He helped to develop a new kind of vessel, the caravel—light, capacious and swift, designed to withstand rough, Atlantic weather, and equipped with movable yards, permitting it to sail *into* the wind.

Henry's caravels brought back ivory and gold dust from Africa, laying the foundations of Portugal's wealth and empire. In Lisbon, he is commemorated by the Monument of the Discoveries—Henry standing at the prow of a huge stone caravel, with the men and women who helped him: mariners, geographers, mathematicians, carpenters, poets.

After Henry, the momentum of discovery did not slacken. Bartolomeu Dias sailed round the boot of Africa; Vasco da Gama came back from India in 1499—with ships dismasted and their crews sick but the holds filled with nutmeg, cloves, cinnamon, pepper and precious stones. (His remains lie in a casket, crowned by soaring gulls' wings, in the city's loveliest monument, the monastery of the Jeronimos.) Pedro Álvares Cabral claimed Brazil for Portugal in 1500, and the Straits of Magellan are named after Ferdinand Magellan, who found them 20 years later.

Christopher Columbus, too, is linked with Lisbon, for he owed everything to it. He landed there in rags, a shipwrecked sailor. He married a Portuguese girl, learned the

*Reminders of times past: nineteenth
century elegance in the main
shopping area; the sixteenth century
Jeronimos monastery; a roof-top
panorama of the Alfama district*

language, and with it the map-making and astronomy essential to navigation; he sailed to Africa and Iceland in Portuguese ships. The story of how he went to Spain and eventually discovered America is well known, but few are aware that his first landfall on the *return* journey was the Portuguese capital.

Great Disaster. With time, how-ever, Lisbon's Golden Age faded, and even its setting was almost wiped out in 1755. On All Saints' Day, November 1, candles blazed in the crowded churches, when sud-denly the city shuddered. Steeples rocked and collapsed, palaces dis-solved, homes disappeared. The great tidal Tagus surged forward. In less than an hour, at least 30,000 people died and one of the Conti-nent's most elegant cities was in ruins. It was the worst earthquake in European history.

Today, the neatly laid-out streets of Lisbon swerve here and there lovingly to preserve an old fountain, a piece of Roman sculpture. Small sections of the old curlicued quarters embellish the new town like ancient baubles. Other relics of the Golden Age are carefully preserved in mu-seums, churches and private homes.

Still, Lisbon remains attached to its past and mourns its losses. There is a word for this sorrow: *saudade*. The closest English equivalent is nos-talgia, a longing for what once ex-isted, a yearning for what will never be again. *Saudade* finds its voice in the *fado*, a lament which is

compounded of Arabic, Negro and Iberian elements, more mournful than the Spanish *flamenco*.

In a hundred dimly-lit *tavernas* and restaurants, the *fado* singers hold forth, moaning of unrequited love, of death and agony on the high seas, of anguish and despair. It is said that the man from Lisbon is happiest when he is weeping. In these cafés a customer starts singing his troubles in the old tidal melody, improvising as he goes along. Then another replies, and still another; and so hours pass in happy melancholy as everybody stows away mountains of the world's best shrimps, spicy charcoal-grilled saus-age and gallons of wine. This is simply one item in the symposium of delights which is Lisbon.

Another is the peculiarly Portu-guese *tourada*, where there are capes but no swords, and where the toreador rides a highly spirited horse, teasing the bull, racing him, dodg-ing his horns in a superb exhibition of horsemanship. After him come the *forcados*, bullfighters in knee breeches and green stocking caps, who line up on foot in the ring and taunt the bull until he charges straight at their leader. The man hurls himself between the animal's horns, wrap-ping his arms around its neck. His companions grab hold wherever they can, until at last the bull has been wrestled to a standstill.

Few countries pay more honour to the saints. Sculptured on house fronts and official buildings you will see a boat with two birds beside it: the symbol of the city's patron, Saint Vincent. Saint Anthony was born in Lisbon and his birthplace is now marked by a church. A statue of Christ, with arms outstretched as if on a cross, dominates the River Tagus on the south bank. The people of Lisbon call it "the traffic cop" but it is a jest flavoured with love. For here religion is not only *observed*; it is a vigorous part of life.

Smack in the middle of the town, near the roaring, singing Rossio Square, always ajam with people sitting in cafés, boys trying to shine your shoes and old men offering you lottery tickets, a lift carries you up 120 feet to Lisbon's hilly heights, where you can stroll through the quaint Bairro Alto district. Once an aristocratic neighbourhood, today it is inhabited by fishermen, sailors and dockers—a soaring annex to the sea, and still one of the most charming parts of Lisbon.

From here you have a splendid view of the lofty St George Castle, dominating the Alfama area which crowds at its feet. This is perhaps the most picturesque quarter of the city. Many houses are splashed with blue or green or yellow, with gables pink and plummy—even the warehouses, where the black gates stand out from peach-stained walls. And above

is the clearest blue sky you've ever seen, partly the result of the climate, partly because the city has so far escaped the pall of industrialization.

Nevertheless, Lisbon is growing fast in area and population. Newly-opened on the Tagus is the world's largest dry dock, capable of handling million-ton ships. Crowded these days with foreign visitors, the city is showing signs of becoming a tourist boom town. The British have been welcomed here since the fourteenth century, when Britain and Portugal were formally linked in a friendship treaty. (Portugal is, in fact, Britain's oldest ally.)

But there's still many a side street that will catapult you back to the Middle Ages. Alleys so narrow that you have to walk single file burst into small flower-bejewelled squares. Old salts, as everyone knows, spend their leisure pottering in gardens, and Lisbon is a paradise of flowers. Even the capital's busy central avenue, the 100-yard-wide Avenida de Liberdade, pauses at two large parks.

A city which laughs at its sorrows, which still broods over its thousand-year-old love-affair with the never-changing sea is likely to remain unique and endearing, even in a world that daily grows more uniform and unremarkable.

THIS ARTICLE FIRST APPEARED IN READER'S DIGEST, JUNE 1972. PHOTOGRAPHS: PAGES 52 AND 53 (RIGHT), FOTOBANK/ ENGLAND SCENE; (INSET LEFT), MICHAEL BOYS/SUSAN GRIGGS AGENCY; PAGE 55, PICTOR INTERNATIONAL; (TOP), ALAIN LE GARSMEUR/IMPACT PHOTOS

Tick-Talk

CUSTOMER, looking at alarm clock, to salesman: "I want one that rings once and gives up."

—Joe Mirachi in *The Wall Street Journal*

The Deer That Went Home to China

BY NIGEL SITWELL

Nearly 90 years after the last native *milu* died out, a British peer has helped reintroduce the species

ON A nippy afternoon in November 1985, some 200 people gathered expectantly near a bamboo-walled hut in a large field on the outskirts of Peking. In the group were farmers, leading Chinese scientists and VIPs including the Marquess of Tavistock, son of the thirteenth Duke of Bedford.

This was a special occasion—the return of a legendary native

Far left: A milu stag guards his does at Woburn. Left: Feeding time in the quarantine hut. Below: Release in Peking's Nan Haizi Milu Park

species to its natural habitat 87 years after its disappearance from the Chinese mainland. The animals, known in China as *milu* (pronounced "meeloo"), literally a deer that lives in swampy places, and to Westerners as Père David's deer, had been donated by Lord Tavistock from the captive herd at Woburn Abbey, Bedfordshire.

Finally, the doors of the hut were pulled open. A head peered out. The animal took a few hesitant steps, looked around with a puzzled air and headed off past the row of spectators. Soon others followed. Within a few minutes, 19 deer had safely left the quarantine hut and disappeared in the direction of a large shallow lake.

It was an emotional homecoming. "I feel very excited and touched," admitted Lord Tavistock. "Returning a herd of these deer to their homeland is something I have wanted to do ever since my grandfather first told me their story when I was about 13."

Milu is a large animal. A mature male weighs between 450 and 550 pounds and stands about four foot six inches at the shoulders. In summer, the animal is reddish brown in colour, turning to greyish brown in winter.

The species was completely unknown outside China until 1865, when its existence was revealed by a French missionary and naturalist, Père Armand David. The vast Imperial Hunting Park, a nearly 145-square-mile preserve near the city of Peking, was surrounded by a high wall. Père David was very curious to find out what animals lived there.

One day he noticed a large heap of sand that had been left by some workmen. Scrambling up the sand and looking over the wall, he saw in the distance "a herd of more than 100 of these animals, which looked like reindeer."

Père David wanted to obtain skins of the unusual creatures for scientific

Lord Tavistock scans deer stock records in the Chinese drawing-room at Woburn

examination, but attempts through the French legation were fruitless. "Luckily I knew some Tartar soldiers who do guard duty in this park," he wrote to Professor Henri Milne-Edwards, who at that time was the director of the Museum of Natural History in Paris. "By means of a bribe I shall get hold of a few skins, which I shall hasten to send to you."

And so he did. A midnight rendezvous was arranged, and the skins and bones of a male and a female were passed over the wall in exchange for 20 silver pieces. The specimens were soon on their way to France. Once the secret was out, strangely enough, the Chinese authorities subsequently complied with requests for live deer and a number were acquired by European zoos.

It appears that the species was almost extinct in the wild for 900 years when the missionary "discovered" it. One difficulty in checking past records stems from one of the Chinese names for the animal, *sibu-xiang*. This means "four unlikes," and refers to the antlers of a deer, the tail of a donkey, the neck of a camel and the hoofs of an ox. This same name was given to some other odd-looking creatures, such as the reindeer and the moose, creating an impression that the deer was more widespread than it really was.

Like the bear, the deer was considered by the Chinese nobility as an animal worthy of hunting, which no doubt explains why it lingered on in deer parks long after it had ceased to exist in the wild. Two events caused its final disappearance. In 1894 the walls of the Imperial Hunting Park were breached by a severe flood and many of the deer escaped into the surrounding countryside, where they were killed by the starving peasants. Six years later, the remainder were completely wiped out during the bloody Boxer Rebellion.

At that point, Herbrand, eleventh Duke of Bedford and Lord Tavistock's great-grandfather, appeared on the scene. A keen naturalist, he realized that the captive Père David's deer in Europe were now the sole survivors of the species. He reckoned that they would be better off if allowed the freedom of a large park, rather then being confined in city zoos. So he acquired all 18 of the deer and released them among 3,000 rolling acres of wooded grassland at Woburn, guarded by a 13-mile wall.

The deer thrived in their new home and continued to do so under the care of Herbrand's son, Hastings. In due course Woburn and its deer passed to the thirteenth Duke, who later transferred the estate to his son, Lord Tavistock. Over the years, groups of the deer have been sent to zoos around the world, and the total population now stands at more than 1,500. The 600 or more at Woburn still constitute by far the largest herd and the only one that is free-ranging.

With such a flourishing herd, Lord Tavistock responded positively to tentative Chinese enquiries in 1980 about the possibility of reintroducing the species. Serious discussions began in the spring of 1984. Bearing the brunt of these negotiations was a long-time friend of Lord Tavistock, Maja Boyd, a 43-year-old American zoologist who had been studying Père David's deer at Woburn Abbey since 1978 and is now helping the Chinese to manage the reintroduced herd.

In 1985, negotiations were finally concluded. More than £450,000 was granted to the project by the Chinese authorities in the first year, followed by an additional sum of £280,000 in 1986. Substantial support has also been provided by several corporations, including Shell Oil (China) and

Connecticut-based Lindblad Travel. In addition, a Chinese non-governmental Milu Foundation to raise funds for the protection and study of the deer brought a quick response. Within a few weeks of the deer's return more than £10,000 had been raised. Among the first donors was a seven-year-old girl who gave her savings from three years' pocket money.

The site chosen for reintroduction is part of a farm and occupies what was formerly the south-western part of the Imperial Hunting Park. The farmers willingly agreed to hand over some 220 acres for the deer's new home, and this, together with another 220 acres of marshland allocated by the government, is now called the Peking Nan Haizi Milu Park, after the shallow lake that occupies part of the area.

Once the final go-ahead was given for the project, workers at the farm moved fast to plant grass and remove part of a tree nursery. Wells were dug and electricity installed. An eight-foot-high wall was built around the outside of the park. Meanwhile, across the world, the deer were being captured at Woburn Abbey. After a month in quarantine, the animals were shipped by air to Peking and loaded on to lorries for the final leg of their journey to Nan Haizi.

One of the aims of the Nan Haizi project is to build up the size of the herd so there are animals available for release in other suitable areas of the country. In the mean time, the project has already produced some significant spin-offs. Birds are appearing within the park that were not there before. And soon after the deer's release, there were plans to enlarge Nan Haizi and develop the region into a green belt.

The object is not just to benefit the deer but to encourage conservation in general. Thus, what began as a unique attempt to return Père David's deer to their homeland may yet turn out to be a catalyst for increasing awareness throughout China of the need to safeguard the good earth and all its wild creatures.

© 1986 NIGEL SITWELL. CONDENSED FROM SMITHSONIAN (JUNE 1986), WASHINGTON DC.
PHOTOGRAPHS: © MICHAEL FREEMAN

Eye-Catcher

WHEN I was offered a freelance assignment, my boss asked me to name my fee and agreed to the modest figure I suggested. As I rose to leave, he said, "In future, when negotiating a fee, always adopt the Blink Principle."

He explained: "Name a figure and watch your prospective employer's face closely to see if he blinks. If not, quickly add, 'That doesn't include my travel expenses, of course.' Still no blink? Follow it with increases for telephone calls, stationery and so on, until he *does* blink. Then stop—you have reached the amount you should have asked for in the first place."

—H. A. B. Mauve, Cape Town, South Africa

How Healthy Are Health Foods?

BY DONALD AND DIANA STROETZEL

BENT on achieving a healthier life-style, Alan and Margaret Smith have said goodbye to fried bacon and eggs for breakfast. They now begin each day with muesli soaked in semi-skimmed milk, fresh fruit and wholemeal toast with additive-free jam or marmalade.

Two or three times a week they eat fish or meat, from which Margaret removes all the fat before cooking. Instead of serving pastry or ice-cream, she may cook a fresh-fruit crumble, made with wholemeal flour and a sprinkling of unrefined sugar. Because she frowns on fatty school-canteen hamburgers, fish fingers and crisps, her eight-year-old son takes a packed lunch that typically includes a wholemeal-bread cheese or salad sandwich, nuts, an additive-free yoghurt, a piece of fruit and a cereal snack-bar.

According to converts like Alan and Margaret, health foods are just the fare to go with cycling, yoga, football and other building blocks of personal fitness. "We've never been healthier," purrs Alan, convinced their son has fewer colds and better teeth than others in the street.

The Smiths are not alone in their enthusiasm for the so-called "health foods." More than a million and a half people in this country are now vegetarians, some of them "vegans" who avoid not only meat but also animal products like milk, cheese, butter and eggs. A recent Gallup poll shows that one in three Britons have reduced their consumption of red meat, and public concern is mounting about excessive sugar and salt in food and the use of chemical additives to preserve and colour fruits, vegetables, meat and drinks.

Profit-Making. No longer is the health-food shop a back-street oddity frequented by eccentrics. In London and the South-East alone there are more than 1,000 outlets. Sometimes charging double the supermarket prices for similar food, they have an annual turnover of £140 million. Says Professor John Dickerson, a University of Surrey nutritionist: "Health food is one of the fastest growing businesses in Britain, reflecting today's intense popular interest in managing one's own health."

Not surprisingly, the pharmaceutical and supermarket chains are beginning to ride the boom. Boots the Chemist promotes health foods in more than 200 of its stores. Even the doughnuts you buy there are wholemeal, their jam fillings free of refined sugar. Meanwhile, supermarkets are pushing low-fat yoghurt and whole-grain muesli cereals.

Back to Nature. Safeway sell organic fruit and vegetables at all their 126 stores, where customers willingly pay extra for Jerusalem artichokes, red cabbage, apples and other vegetables and fruits grown without chemical fertilizers. Demand has been so heavy that the chain can't buy enough in Britain. Sixty per cent come from the Continent and as far away as Israel.

"A splendid opportunity for British farmers," says Sue Hill, marketing adviser for the National Farmers' Union. Illustrating what can be done, 38-year-old Dutch immigrant Dirk Bauer has built a yoghurt factory on his 152 acres of pasture outside East Grinstead. His 35 cows feed on grass fertilized entirely with manure. Their milk brings him 48 pence per half kilo as organic yoghurt contracted to supermarkets—some six times what he would get from the Milk Marketing Board for bulk whole milk.

How do Britain's health professionals view this swelling love-affair? Many health-food offerings are directly in line with the key recommendations of NACNE—the National Advisory Committee on Nutrition Education.

In a bold attempt to reduce

cholesterol levels, believed to be a major cause of coronary-artery disease, NACNE urges a 25-per-cent cut in fat consumption, particularly of saturated fat. Health foods replace saturated-fat red meat and dairy products with nutrient-rich beans, other vegetables and fruit. There is even cow's milk in which polyunsaturated sunflower oil is substituted for dairy fat, reducing saturated-fat content from 14 grams per pint to a mere 0·3.

Another NACNE recommendation is to eat less salt, less sugar. High-sodium food raises blood pressure in some people, while sugar is a villain in tooth decay. Health-food stores offer a range of low-salt, low-sugar foods. But be wary. The sweetening in health foods is often provided by honey—as bad for teeth as sugar.

Roughage Value. NACNE also urges us to eat more fibre because water-absorbing fibre softens the faeces, speeding transit through the bowels. That means less time for bacteria and carcinogens from food to interact with the colon's mucous membranes. Doctors think this may reduce the risks of diseases such as colon cancer. The health-food stores make fibre-eating easy with dried apricots and figs, exotic beans, and whole-grain breads containing twice to three times the fibre of white.

On the other hand, doctors put little stock in claimed health-food "cures" for disease. Cider vinegar, for example, is touted for high blood pressure, dizziness, sore throats, obesity and varicose veins. A herbal tablet is promoted for complaints from constipation to appendicitis. "Do you really believe that 25 different illnesses can be cured by one small pill?" asks Professor Arnold Bender, author of *Health or Hoax?*

Some "natural" remedies like "extract of green-lipped New Zealand mussel," taken to relieve the stiffness and pain of arthritis, have at least had clinical tests with results suggesting they may help. But many have no more substantiation than old wives' tales. While generally harmless biologically, they can lure the sick away from proper medical treatment.

Health-professional opinion is divided about two other props of the health food business: organically grown food free from chemicals, and vegetarianism. According to the Ministry of Agriculture, Fisheries and Food, which regularly analyses food samples, there is no nutritional difference between foods grown with animal manure and those fertilized with chemicals.

"On the other hand," says Dr John Brown, nutritionist with the Health Education Council, "we simply don't know the health risks of very small traces of pesticides often found on fruits and vegetables."

But can we be sure that "organically grown vegetables" really *are* free of harmful chemicals? When a California laboratory analysed 28 samples of "organic" vegetables and fruits from health-food stores in the US and 14 similar but non-organic items from supermarkets, only two were free of pesticide residues—and one of those was from a non-organic supermarket. In Britain, guidelines for growing food organically are produced by the Soil Association, but grower compliance is voluntary.

Hidden Danger. When it comes to food processing, permitted additives are strictly controlled by Ministry regulations to avoid any that might pose a health threat. Yet occasionally there's a case like that of 13-year-old Orion Wilson, of Chertsey, Surrey. Subject to violent mood shifts, he constantly disrupted classes at school. But he calmed down dramatically when his parents put him on foods free from chemical additives. He was allergic to several additives including tartrazine, a colouring agent that some doctors link with hyperactivity in children.

While most health authorities agree that there is little to be said for colouring agents, few would favour an outright ban on chemical preservatives. Better to diagnose and treat the rare allergy case caused by preservatives, they say, than to deprive millions of year-round cheaper food.

Vegetarians are only a shade less controversial. They claim to offset their high outlays for health food by not eating expensive meat. After counting lifetime days spent in hospitals by 75 vegetarians versus 75 non-vegetarians of all ages, randomly selected, the University of Surrey's Professor Dickerson considers that vegetarians are healthier. The non-vegetarians reported nearly five times as many hospital days, with a cost to the NHS of £60,000 as against £12,000 for the vegetarians.

But Dr John Catford, professor of health education at University of Wales College of Medicine, worries that without meat, vegetarians may not get enough B-complex vitamins, iron and zinc. And if they eat more high-fat dairy products like eggs and cheese as alternatives to meat, they may consume *more* saturated fats than meat-eaters.

The traditional meat and two vegetables provide a balanced meal that is relatively easy to prepare. To obtain equivalent nutrients without meat requires a more complicated combination of pulses, cereals, nuts and seeds.

The truth about health foods is probably best summed up by the Health Education Council's Dr Brown. "Eaten sensibly, pretty well all food is healthy," he says, "and it is certainly true that a little of what you fancy does you good. The unique contribution of health-food shops is to put variety and interesting new tastes into the food that does you *most* good."

PHOTOGRAPH: PETER HIGGINS, MATERIAL SUPPLIED BY ALARA WHOLE FOODS

Purse Strings

OFFICE sign: "The Golden Rule: He who holds the gold makes the rules."

—A. L. Girling

Towards More Picturesque Speech

Full Blast

The winter wind is a lonely wind; a frigid, invisible force on a desperate mission to nowhere, wailing and shrieking and leaving behind a trail of frozen grass and naked trees shivering in the cold light of the moon, as it sweeps across the land without a backward glance   —O. T.

Die Hards

Old bankers never die; they just yield to maturity   —Susan Weschler

Old lecturers never die; they know they'll see better dais   —Shelby Friedman

Old dictators never die; they just fly the coup   —C. P. Miscavish

Old lawyers never die—they just lose their appeal   —Bob Talbert in Detroit *Free Press*

Things of Beauty

Patches of happiness in the quilt of life
                                            —Dale Dimos

Dark-velvet silence   —Mrs L. Black

A day that stepped out of the calendar wearing new shoes   —Margaret Runbeck

Did You Hear About…

…the pianist who took a nocturne for the worse?

…the flute player who discovered there's gold in them thar trills?   —S F.

Place Settings

Venetian rivalry: doge eat doge
                —A. H. Berzen in *The Wall Street Journal*

Blarney Stone: sham rock   —Ron Zeh

Tower of Babel: din of iniquity
                        —quoted by Bob Phillips

Siberia: the Red barren   —Arthur Ruh

Easy Felines

As busy as a box of kittens
            —Griffin Smith in *National Geographic*

A swing seat cradling a puddle of cat
                        —Gloria Schlesna

Two black cats, lying like inverted commas on the sofa   —Jay Smedley

We pay £25 or more for an item for "Towards More Picturesque Speech." See page 1 for details.

CHRISTO
Wrap-Around Artist

BY ROBERT WERNICK

His crazy projects cause alarm, outrage and delight

As the full moon rose over Paris, Christo paced the deck of a barge moored downstream from the bridge that, a few days earlier, he had wrapped in 50,000 square yards of golden-yellow nylon fabric. With his slight frame, bony animated face and dark eyes flashing under a safety helmet, he looked like Napoleon at Austerlitz.

As on a battlefield, a stream of couriers arrived at his command post with the latest dispatches. "Christo," cried one of them, "I've just heard on the radio that more than a million people have already come to see your bridge." "Christo,"

Parcelling up the Pont-Neuf: Christo (centre) directs operations

implored another, "come and look at the moon."

Christo hastened to the stern of the barge. The moon had cleared the towers of Notre Dame and was bathing the banks of the Seine in its splendour. Filtered through the pollution of the city air, it had taken on a rich golden hue, the exact colour of the material in which the bridge was wrapped. "Get my photographer at once," commanded Christo, smiling as he savoured the one moment since time began that the moon and the Pont-Neuf were the same colour— Christo's colour.

That September evening in 1985, he had every reason to be elated. Twenty-seven years before, Christo Javacheff, a penniless refugee from Bulgaria, had walked the streets of Paris worrying how to pay his rent. Now Christo, a world-famous artist, the notorious Wrapman, had wrapped the city's oldest and most illustrious bridge.

Like all Christo's projects, this one was the fruit of years of planning. He had always dreamed of producing a piece of public art in the city where his artistic career had taken shape. It was in Paris, in 1962, that people first became aware of Christo's work when he erected a wall of oil drums across a narrow street in the Latin Quarter—his ironic commentary on the Berlin Wall. Since then he had moved his headquarters to New York. But he often thought about returning to Paris in style.

His first idea had been to wrap all

Parisians crowded to admire their new-look bridge

the trees on the Champs-Elysées. Permission was refused by the city authorities. Then he thought of the Pont-Neuf, a seventeenth century architectural masterpiece. Millions of tourists, strollers and lovers have leaned on its parapets to watch the Seine glide by. Thousands of Parisians cross it every day. What better place for Christo to wrap?

In 1975 he began with a detailed

Christo used almost 23 acres of fabric to wrap three miles of Australian coastline

study of the paintings, drawings and architectural renderings of the site in the archives. Photographs were taken of the bridge from dozens of angles, and he drew and painted over them, pasting together collages to see how different wrappings would look.

Such work is only the beginning of a Christo project. "My art," he likes to say, "is meant to impinge directly on people's daily lives." And that it does. Every announcement of a Christo project stirs up waves of incomprehension and curiosity.

The artist had to convince the prickly neighbours of the Pont-Neuf that what he was designing was not going to hurt them but might add an element of excitement to their lives. In autumn 1981, doorbells began ringing as young women devoted to Christo's art answered questions and distributed literature. Soon everyone within a third of a mile of the bridge knew what was afoot. Then Christo came in person. In his rapid-fire, ungrammatical but fluent French, his unkempt black locks flying, he poured out his ideas.

He belongs, he explained, to a current in the contemporary art world that rejects the traditional notion that art is only something to be put on gallery walls or on pedestals. It can also be part of ordinary life.

Christo's art takes many forms, but his speciality is wrapping. When you offer a gift to someone, you generally have it wrapped first, to endow it with an extra dimension of mystery. Like the dress a designer fashions, it is meant to emphasize what it seems to conceal.

So, when Christo wraps a piece of natural scenery, as he did three miles of rocky coastline in Australia in 1969, or when he wraps a public monument like the statue of Leonardo da Vinci in Milan (1970), or when he surrounds 11 islands off Miami with pink plastic (1983) and stretches 22,000 square yards of nylon across a Colorado valley (1970-72), he is calling attention to things that are grandiose and beautiful, but so familiar that people tend to take them for granted.

Package Deal. "Thousands of you pass the Pont-Neuf every day," Christo said to Parisians, "but how many actually *see* it, stop to appreciate it? Just by being there for a couple of weeks, my fabric wrapping will add a new dimension to the bridge. Long after it is removed, people passing by will remember Christo and will look more keenly and fondly at the splendid stones."

A Christo idea tends to be very expensive. Workers' wages, material costs, insurance and lawyers' fees can reach £2 million, as they did for the Pont-Neuf. How does an artist raise this kind of money? He sells the myriad sketches, drawings and scale models that form the gestation phase of each project, and which collectors and museums are glad to grab for

anything from £15,000 to £65,000.

So successful has this tactic been that Christo's projects have always been paid off to the penny, though the Christo family has often had to worry about paying the rent. "Every penny we make goes straight into the next project," says his French-born wife Jeanne-Claude cheerfully.

Red Tape. Any scheme involving tons of equipment and hundreds of people is bound to encounter plenty of hitches—especially administrative ones. Wrapping the Pont-Neuf was no exception. Although the Christos got the enthusiastic support of the French Minister of Culture, the Paris police were concerned about public safety and the traffic flow; the electricity board worried about their wiring.

It took six years to get approval from the Mayor of Paris, Jacques Chirac. And it was not until July 1985 that President Mitterrand gave his assent.

No one before Christo had ever wrapped a bridge, so every detail of the operation had to be thought out from scratch. What material should be used? It had to be strong, fireproof, easy to clean. A thick nylon cloth made in Germany was eventually chosen. What colour should it be? Christo settled on the golden tone that blended with the sandstone of the old buildings in Paris.

Every one of the Pont-Neuf's 12 arches differs in dimension and degree of curvature. The cloth had to fit without sagging and be attached to the bridge in such a way that not one of the ancient stones was chipped or scraped. And it had to be put on without disrupting the 24-hour-a-day flow of traffic.

Solving these problems took the collaboration of hundreds of workers, professionals and volunteers. Familiar figures from previous Christo projects turned up from all over the globe, like Ted Dougherty, a building contractor from Colorado, who spent six months working out every detail of the project to the last inch. Craftsmen had to be found to cut and sew the cloth, ropemakers for the cables that would hold it in place, carpenters to build the framework of wood and steel to protect the stones from being scratched when the cloth was tightened into place.

French Dressing. The original plan had been to drape the bridge using bulky cranes. A more elegant solution was worked out: the fabric was accordion-pleated in giant protective cocoons, placed under the bridge on barges, lifted up over the balustrades and secured with heavy ballast. Alpine guides and tree pruners were hired to scamper up the vertical surfaces of the Pont-Neuf's piers and arches with the ropes; professional scuba divers took care of the underwater anchoring.

At dusk on September 15, to the cheers of delighted crowds on both banks of the river, the fabric began to rise in majestic golden bands. It took five days to get it all in place, attached to supporting steel cables and tied with 43,000 feet of rope.

The critics raved, Parisians loved it, and 750,000 free samples of the wrapping were handed out to people who wanted to remember what the Pont-Neuf had looked like during the two blissful weeks the display was up.

Today the Christos are back in New York, and new ideas are flowing at the usual breakneck pace. Will Christo be allowed to wrap the immense Reichstag building in Berlin? The Mayor of Berlin is in favour; Chancellor Kohl is still putting off a decision. The Russians have occupation rights to one wall of the building. What will they say?

Then there is his scheme to unfurl banners to wave ten feet above the 27 miles of footpath in New York's Central Park. City officials produced a 209-page document saying it was in effect impractical, undesirable and impertinent—"the longest way to say 'No,'" says Christo, "in the annals of art." But he is confident that when he has had a chance to speak to New Yorkers, even the city fathers will end up saying "Yes" to Christo the Wrapman.

PHOTOGRAPHS: WOLFGANG VOLZ; PAGE 71, HARRY SHUNK

Far-Sighted

NATURE is wonderful. A million years ago she didn't know we were going to need glasses, but look where she put our ears.   —Los Angeles Times Syndicate

CONVECTED AIR FROM THE GRILLE SENDS WARMTH RIGHT ROUND THE ROOM.

A NEW GAS FIRE. WELCOMING, CONTROLLABLE

YOU'LL COME HOME TO A WARM WELCOME
WHATEVER THE WEATHER.

WITH A WIDE RANGE
OF DESIGNS TO CHOOSE
FROM, YOU'LL FIND
A GAS FIRE TO SUIT
YOUR HOME EXACTLY.

THIS IS THE CANNON FLAME 5. ONE OF THE WID
YOU'LL FIND AT YOUR BRITISH

SETTLE FOR A GAS FIRE
AND SETTLE DOWN IN LUXURY.

GAS. NO WONDER

ALL THE BEAUTY OF AN OPEN FIRE BUT
WITHOUT THE INCONVENIENCE –
OR THE HEAT LOSS.

OU'LL FILL YOUR
OOM WITH WARMTH
N MINUTES.

HEAT AT THE HEART OF YOUR HOME,

YOU'RE ALWAYS
COMFORTABLY IN CONTROL.

WARMTH WITH ECONOMY –
THAT'S THE BEAUTY OF GAS.

NGE OF BEAUTIFUL FIRES
S SHOWROOM.

ISN'T IT TIME YOU CAME HOME TO THE COMFORT OF A NEW GAS FIRE?

PEOPLE PREFER IT.

British Gas
ENERGY IS OUR BUSINESS

One day son, all this won't be yours

For 25 years, the British Heart Foundation has been funding vital research into Britain's biggest killer, heart disease.

We've achieved a great deal already. But we need your help if we're to continue building a healthier, safer world for the next generation to grow up in.

The more you help us, the more we'll find out.

Women Who Love Too Much

BY ROBIN NORWOOD

It's not just bad luck that draws them into damaging relationships

I N THE fairy-tale "Beauty and the Beast," a young girl meets a frightening monster. To save her family from his wrath, she agrees to live with him. Eventually, by getting to know him, she overcomes her loathing and even grows to love him. A miracle occurs, and he is restored to his true, princely self.

This *seems* to underscore a cultural assumption that we can change someone for the better through the force of our love, and that, if we are female, it is our duty to do so.

When a woman doesn't like many of a man's basic characteristics, values and modes of behaviour, but puts up with them thinking that if she is only loving enough he'll want to change, she is loving too much.

I recognized the phenomenon of "loving too much" as a specific syndrome of thoughts, feelings and behaviour after several years of counselling alcohol and drug abusers. Sometimes the patients I interviewed grew up in troubled families, but their partners *nearly always* came from severely disturbed families. By struggling to cope with their addictive mates, these partners were unconsciously re-creating and reliving significant aspects of their childhood.

The wives and girlfriends of addictive men revealed their need for both the superiority and the suffering they experienced in their "saviour" role. These women clarified for me the incredible power and influence their childhood experiences had on their adult patterns of relating to men.

Women are not, of course, the only ones who love too much. Some men practise this obsession with as much fervour as any woman could, and their feelings and behaviour issue from the same kinds of childhood experiences. However, most men who have been damaged in childhood tend not to develop an addiction to relationships. Because of an interplay of cultural and biological factors, they usually try to protect themselves and avoid their pain through an obsession with work, sport or hobbies.

Thousands of women choose partners who are indifferent, abusive, cruel, emotionally unavailable, addictive or otherwise unable to be loving and caring. No one becomes such a woman—a woman who loves too much—by accident. There are no accidents in marriage.

When a woman believes that she inexplicably "had to get married" to a certain man, or claims she married on whim, or that she was too young to know what she was doing, it is imperative for her to examine why she chose that particular man. For she *did* choose, albeit unconsciously, and often with a wealth of knowledge about him even at the outset.

Many women make the mistake of looking for a man without first developing a relationship with themselves. No one can ever love us enough to fulfil us if we do not love ourselves. When in our emptiness we go looking for love, we can only find more emptiness.

Consider the case of Peggy, a divorced single parent with two daughters:

My father and mother separated before I was born, and my mother went to work while her mother took care of us. My grandmother was a terribly cruel woman who would always tell us we were "good for nothing."

Her criticisms made my sister and me try harder to be good, to be worthwhile. My mother never protected us; she was too afraid Grandma would leave and there would be no one to take care of us. I remember I used to try to mend things that broke around the house, wanting to save us money and earn my keep somehow.

I married at 18. I met my husband at school. He was lounging against a wall when he should have been in class. I thought, "He looks pretty wild; I bet I could settle him down." I was still trying to fix things. I was miserable from the start, but it took me 15 years to believe that being miserable was a good enough reason to get a divorce.

After the divorce, I met Baird. He was tall and very good-looking. But he also had an air of coldness about him. I remember telling myself, "That is the most elegant, arrogant man I've ever seen. I bet I could warm him up!" We never did have a really good time together. Something was always wrong, and I kept trying to make it right. Our marriage lasted only two months.

Peggy knew nothing about being loved. So strong was her need to replicate the hostile environment of her childhood and continue her struggle to win love from those who could not give it that when she met a man who struck her as being cold, aloof and indifferent, she was instantly attracted to him. Here was another opportunity to change an unloving person into someone who would finally love her.

Once they became involved with each other, she kept trying in spite of the devastation to her own life. Her need to change him (and her mother and grandmother, who he represented) was that strong.

In dysfunctional families, major aspects of reality are denied, and roles remain rigid. This severely impairs the development of our basic tools for living and for relating to people and situations.

It is this basic impairment that operates in women who love too much. They become unable to discern when someone or something is not good for them. The situations and people that others would naturally avoid as dangerous, uncomfortable or unwholesome do not repel them, because they do not trust or even know their feelings. Instead, they are actually drawn to the very dangers, intrigues and challenges that others would avoid. Through this attraction they are further damaged, because much of what they are attracted to is

a replication of what they lived with growing up. They get hurt all over again.

Consider Chloe, a 23-year-old university student:

When I was young my father hit my mother. He hit all us kids. I suppose he sort of convinced us that we deserved to be beaten. But I knew Mum didn't. I always wished he'd hit me instead of her. I knew I could take it, and I wasn't so sure she could. We all wanted Mum to leave him, but she wouldn't. I wanted to give her enough love to make her strong so she could get out; she never did. She died of cancer five years ago. I haven't spoken to my father since then.

I met Roy on an art course. One day he started talking about women being totally spoilt, and how they just used men. He was dripping with venom as he spoke, and I thought, "Oh, he's really been hurt." I began trying to prove to him that women weren't all like that.

In less than two months, we were living together. In four months, I was paying the rent and almost every other bill. But I kept trying, for two more years, to prove how I wasn't going to hurt him the way he'd already been hurt, to prove that he was lovable. I got hurt quite a bit in the process, at first just emotionally, then physically. Of course, I felt that was my fault, too. It's a miracle I got out. I met a former girlfriend of his, and she asked me, straight out, "Does he ever hit you?"

We talked a long time. She got me

79

to go with her to a therapy group she was in, and I think it probably saved my life. Those women were just like me. They had learnt to put up with incredible amounts of pain, usually starting in childhood.

Children inevitably carry the guilt and blame for serious problems that affect their families. Their fantasy of omnipotence makes them believe both that they are the cause of the families' circumstances and that they have the power to change them.

A woman who habitually practises denial and control will be drawn into situations demanding those traits. Denial, by keeping her out of touch with the reality of her circumstances and her feelings, will lead her into relationships fraught with difficulty. She will then employ all her skills at helping/controlling in order to make the situation more tolerable, all the while denying how bad it really is.

It is not easy or comfortable for us to consider that selfless behaviour, "being good," and efforts to help may actually be attempts to control, to change others. When we do for another what he can do for himself, when we prompt, advise, remind, cajole another person who is not a young child—this is controlling. Our hope is that if we can control him, then we can control our own feelings where our life touches his. And of course the harder we try to control him, the less we are able to.

SO WHAT, then, is the point of "Beauty and the Beast?" It is acceptance—the antithesis of denial and control. It is a willingness to recognize what reality is and to allow that reality to be, without a need to change it. Beauty loved the Beast. Therein lies a happiness that issues not from manipulating outside conditions or people, but from developing inner peace, even in the face of challenges and difficulties.

Ironically, it is this very practice of acceptance that allows another to change if he chooses to do so. Remember, Beauty did not try to make a prince out of a monster. Because of her acceptance, he was freed to become his own best self.

CONDENSED FROM "WOMEN WHO LOVE TOO MUCH." © 1985 ROBIN NORWOOD. PUBLISHED BY ARROW BOOKS

Winter Woollies

FARMERS in Britain are wrapping up their sheep in overcoats to keep them warm and dry through the winter. The indignity for an industry which encourages people to wear expensive sheepskin coats to keep warm is that the new garments are woven from man-made fibre. They are light, waterproof and cost only £2 each.

The lightweight coats are claimed to have resulted in cleaner, drier fleeces, healthier sheep and lambs. Lambs can shelter underneath their mothers' overcoats for warmth, and it is claimed the death-rate among newborn lambs and newly shorn sheep has fallen. —David Brown in *Sunday Telegraph*

Buy-Lines
by Madeleine MacDonnell

I've got a total of 8½ pages for you this month. As well as this one, there's page 94, Hints for your Home starting on page 16 and Holiday Ideas from page 169 on.

"Warning. This property protected by ultra-violet security" are words that will make thieves think twice—and probably try elsewhere. They appear on the window stickers that are part of the **Securikit**. Also included are two "invisible" markers with which to mark your property; a battery-operated ultra-violet *Securilite* with which you'll be able to see and check your security coding; 4 window and 10 individual-warning stickers; 4 Duracell batteries and a zip-up PVC case. Police forces are now equipped with ultra-violet lights so lost or stolen property can be easily identified and returned once it is Securikit code marked. Write your post code and house number on everything you own—preferably on an area that will not be exposed to daylight, such as the base of a vase. These identifying marks *can not be removed* by any of the usual household cleaners nor will they show.

The complete Securikit costs just £17.95 including p&p. Get it by sending your name and address and a cheque/PO payable to Reader's Digest to: **Buy-Lines, 25 Berkeley Square, London W1X 6AB.** (Or use the coupon on page 11). Please allow 14 days for delivery.

Reg No 340452 England

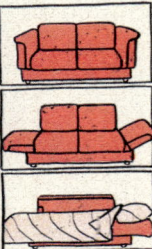

Buying a suite of furniture represents a major purchase for most of us. Making the wrong choice could prove to be an expensive mistake. So **Parker Knoll** have produced a book to help you choose with more confidence the style and design of settee or chair that best suits you. They make furniture to suit every life style and offer a choice of more than 120 fabrics and 13 different wood finishes. Browse through the book in your own home (to get a copy, free, put **69** on the coupon) then try each chair for yourself at your local Parker Knoll showroom.

Bad backs often equate with bad beds, so the bed you sleep on could be the cause of your back pains. The answer is to have your bed tailor-made for you and you alone. Every bed that **OBAS**, the orthopaedic bed specialists, make is made to suit the person who is to sleep on it. His or her height, weight and medical history are taken into account and, where it's a double bed, *each side* is tailor-made. OBAS make all their beds themselves which gives them complete control of quality and cost. Ask for details now by putting **68** on the coupon on page 11.

Can you manage the stairs? Anyone can glide up and down the stairs at the touch of a button, and in complete safety, on a **Stannah Stairlift**. You regain the full use of your home and it's much less of an upheaval than re-arranging your house to one-floor living or moving home. A Stannah is installed in less than a day, with no mess, to straight or curved staircases and, when not in use, it folds back out of the way. Get full details and find out about how you can have a free demonstration of a Stannah Stairlift by putting **72** on the coupon on page 11 now.

Knit yourself a masterpiece for under £30! The beautiful sweater that you can see on page 24, designed by Susan Duckworth, is available in a *knitting kit* from **Ehrman's**. Each kit contains the pattern and all the yarn (100% double knitting wool) you need to knit sizes 32" to 38"—you supply the needles. Any averagely experienced knitter can make this Pink Basketweave sweater and, having seen it made up, I can tell you that it's gorgeous. And just imagine what it would cost you to buy ready hand-knitted!

Order your knitting kit now by using the coupon on page 24.

Apache Raid

BY JOHN PRESCOTT

**Uncle Harlan never cared much for the preacher,
until the day of the chase**

I CAME to live with my Uncle Harlan and Aunt Martha Allen after the massacre, Uncle Harlan being my mother's older brother when she was living. Since our families were among the early settlers in the valley, coming out to Arizona in 1865, their places bordered on each other.

Uncle Harlan sometimes rode over to tend the graves on my folks' place, but I didn't. I was 12 now, but I was still afraid, and didn't want to have so sharp in my mind all I'd seen on that day, or heard or smelt.

Save Tucson, 70 miles around the Santa Rita Mountains, there were no towns in that grassy piece of country. At times a month would pass with no human beings even going by. Seems like the ones we saw most often were travelling preachers. They might show up any time, stopping at each ranch to pray and hymn, maybe baptize a child.

These visits were looked for by Aunt Martha, while Uncle Harlan could take them or leave them. He joked about the preachers. "Feller smells of pulpit clear to here," he would say. Or, "They always come in time to feed, yet they never fill out. A puzzle."

To Aunt Martha, these jokes were blasphemy. She might say, "You're going up in a curl of smoke one of these days. He knows you're mocking him." Then he'd say, "I sometimes question if he knows, or knowing, if he cares. Anna and Harold never mocked him."

As he spoke this way only when he

thought I couldn't hear, it was hard to tell if he was still joking. By his voice, he seemed to be, but he never joked about my folks' being killed. My mother—much younger than he—had been like a daughter to him.

As a rule, the preachers showed up on some stringy nag. But once we had one come afoot. It happened in late summer. The sun was sliding behind the Santa Ritas, and the pasture had that reddish-gold colour of early evening. Then, from off the trail, a man came walking.

"Clark," Uncle Harlan said to me, "get my rifle."

I did, nor did I ask why. In cow country, nothing was more chancy than a man afoot. Moreover, it wasn't long since Uncle Harlan had shot a looter digging in the ruins of my folks' place.

The man was closer now, and we could see his long legs folding and unfolding. His tailcoat drooped down low and his stove-pipe hat stuck high up. Maybe a minute passed before we saw his collar was turned backward. Then Aunt Martha said, "Praise the Lord, it's a preacher."

Pretty soon the man came loping up, bowed and raised his hat. "The name is Obadiah Balk," he declared, "minister of the Gospel, and preacher to the heathen. Friends call me Deacon."

"A deacon!" Aunt Martha began, smoothing her apron. "We've never had a deacon stop before now."

"Preacher to the heathen, you say?" said Uncle Harlan. "The only word them butchers savvy comes from a gun barrel."

The deacon's smile turned holy and full of patience. "The Word is the same for all of God's creatures,"

he said, "for the heathen, as well as those of little faith."

As she couldn't tell how Uncle Harlan might respond, Aunt Martha told the deacon that he'd come in time for supper.

First, we had grace, a long one with flowing words; yet its end left us hanging while the deacon's hand slid out to fork a big slice of chicken breast. Then, along with the rest of the food, a heap of church talk was served. Supper done, the deacon puffed away on one of those cigars Uncle Harlan got from Tucson, and tamped his meal down with a big glass of Uncle Harlan's cherry cordial. Then he led us off on a round of hymns. Aunt Martha's face was filled with pure light.

A week or so passed by and Aunt Martha began to wonder about the deacon coming our way again. "When he finds that nobody else around has cigars like mine," Uncle Harlan said. "Or when he wants a drink of my cordial."

"Now, Harlan, you'd be thirsty, too, if you travelled on foot," Aunt Martha said.

"A man afoot can't be trusted," he retorted, good and riled now.

Aunt Martha's face got red and her voice shook. "I don't think you love us any more," she said. "You wouldn't talk so, if you did."

I'd seen them quarrel before, but not in this way. They waved their arms and sent their voices up. But the worst was feeling that something bigger lay under what they spoke of.

I was glad the cattle round-up was near; it was better to be busy than fretting about Aunt Martha and Uncle Harlan. There was plenty to do: provisions to pack, branding irons to clean, leather to soap.

Then there was the brush pile to be used for signal smoke if Indians came. This was on a hog-back ridge up behind the house where, if it was lit, the men working the round-up on the plains would see it. I always stacked on plenty of green wood, and kept a pail of paraffin handy.

The days being so full, the deacon had grown smaller in my mind. When he came again, a few days before round-up, I was surprised. The first thought was that he might better have come when Uncle Harlan had left. Even from up at my brush pile, their manner of standing said trouble. When I reached them, Uncle Harlan's face looked grumbly, and Aunt Martha's eyes were steamy. The deacon stared at his boots.

Pretty quick, though, the deacon pulled up and smiled. "The heathen will all change when I go among them with the Word," he said.

"Now you bring it up, you might go now," Uncle Harlan said. "But the other thing is out. Nobody's going to turn my sister's place into a church. Ain't no preacher got any business over there after what happened."

"It would make a fine church," said the deacon. "All it needs is a new roof, and God would always be there to talk to."

Uncle Harlan, by now, would

make a range bull look calm. "And a damned sight later than he should have been."

As this was so much worse than all his other blasphemies, Aunt Martha stared as if he was the devil. But not until the deacon had gone and we lay in our beds at night did I hear her say in a thin, splintery voice, "Now, I know what troubles you, Harlan. You've held it in a long time, working. Since Anna and Harold died."

In the darkness, Uncle Harlan's voice came dry and bare, "I don't want to talk about it."

"You don't have to," she said. "It always shows when a body turns his grief on God in anger."

It was out, that dark, strange thing that I had only partly seen. I grew frightened. Uncle Harlan's silence made me see him with a glare of wrath about him as he shook his fist at God.

Round-up came, and Uncle Harlan rode off. He might be gone a week. At home, the time stretched over the frame of days like a drumhead. Each morning before dawn, I'd go to the roof and stand watch. Dawn was the time for Apache raiding parties.

One day towards noon, Aunt Martha busted in from outside. "Get the signal fire going, Clark! There's Indians over the creek!"

I didn't feel the pail slamming my legs or the oil spilling out. No more than I felt the pull of the climb or the ground hitting my feet. My mind was full of Indians.

I didn't look at them until the fire took hold and I'd started down. They were far off, in the hills across the creek. But they looked just as on that day past, making it so true that I could hear the screams, smell the flesh burning, see the blackness of the cellar where I was hidden, and see how humans look when they're ripped open, and all inside comes oozing out.

I was in a state when I reached the house. Aunt Martha jerked me in, slammed the door and drove the bar through the brackets. She put the gun into my hand, and slung the bandoleer of ammunition around my neck; she shoved me towards the ladder. Up on the roof we lay behind the mud parapet and pushed our rifles over the edge.

By now, the Indians weren't so tiny. They were still above the creek, but running in single file. There was something in how they ran—that and the time of day—that didn't square with their known habits on raids, but I couldn't tell until Aunt Martha pointed. "It's the deacon!" she said.

He was out ahead of the Indians, his long legs pumping, and his clothes, except a scrap or two, gone. When I saw his boots were missing, too, I knew what had happened. They did such things, though no one knew why. On finding someone, they'd strip his shoes off, then pointing at the sun, sign that he had so much time before they gave chase. A game it was; a joke before business.

But it was plain they hadn't figured on a walking man, one so leggy. It was plain, too, that he might reach us. Did they catch the deacon, they'd likely leave us be, but given he made the house, we'd be killed, too.

As it turned out, the deacon didn't cross over the creek. When we saw him next, he was far downstream, still on the yon side. He was wobbling now, and the Indians were close behind, yelling wild.

I was still trying to figure out what had happened, when Aunt Martha turned and looked behind us. From the pile of brush, the smoke was lifting into the sky, thick, black and oily. "He saw it," she said. "He knew we were alone, and he kept away."

Uncle Harlan reached us in an hour, his horse caked with foam, its nose running blood. Had Aunt Martha really thought he didn't love us any more, she'd have known different when he hugged us, and the words, when he tried to speak, wouldn't come out right.

When we told what happened, he ran for the creek with a rifle in each hand. He didn't need them, though. By then the Indians had gone.

For a miracle, he found the deacon still living, and that night he rode hard to Fort Lowell, at Tucson, to get the army surgeon. He was back before noon the next day.

When the surgeon had done his work, Aunt Martha held that godliness had saved the deacon's life. But the surgeon wondered if the Indians hadn't let him live because he'd run against them so well. Sometimes they were funny that way. All they'd done was cut those Achilles tendons down by his ankles so that it wouldn't happen again. Sometimes they were funny that way, too.

Coming down to how he kept the Indians away from me and Aunt Martha, though, was something different. Uncle Harlan gave in at last, and spent the rest of that autumn putting up a new roof on my folks' place. I helped him. I found I didn't scare at all over there any more, but liked it.

Nowadays, Uncle Harlan doesn't quarrel with God. Nor does he poke fun at Deacon Obadiah Balk. Each Sunday when the deacon comes riding on his mule, Uncle Harlan is waiting to shoulder him down and help him up to the porch for a smoke and a glass of cordial before dinner.

You might even call them good friends now. But, as Uncle Harlan likes to say, it was almost bound to happen once the deacon took to riding, like any other human being out in cattle country.

CONDENSED FROM SATURDAY EVENING POST (JULY 26, 1958). © 1958 THE SATURDAY EVENING POST CO., INDIANAPOLIS, INDIANA. ILLUSTRATION: PAT OWEN

Sunny Side Up

A HOLIDAY leaflet extolling the virtues of a region in north-west Sicily recommends it particularly "for people searching for transparent bottoms, crystalline seasides and suggestive landscapes." —D. Gardiner, Cardiff

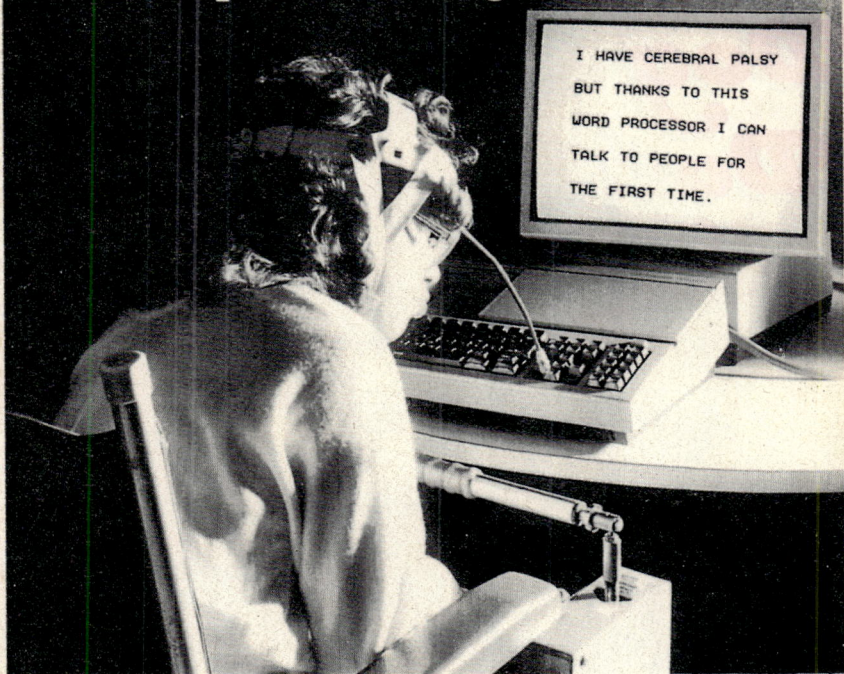

Leave someone the power of speech in your Will.

I HAVE CEREBRAL PALSY BUT THANKS TO THIS WORD PROCESSOR I CAN TALK TO PEOPLE FOR THE FIRST TIME.

Imagine a lively mind imprisoned in a body which cannot perform even a simple function like speech.

This is the frustrating plight of many people with cerebral palsy (spasticity).

Using the latest communications technology (and a lot of old-fashioned patience and care) The Spastics Society can often help them to make real contact with other people for the first time in their lives.

But without your support, we cannot do nearly enough.

Just think for a moment how many everyday activities which you take for granted are denied to severely disabled people – and how much your legacy can help provide them with the practical help they need and deserve.

Dog Days

"You spoil that chihuahua."

"He's very gentle, but prey to
uncontrollable fits of the giggles."

"I must say, Mr Baskerville, we had expected something larger."

"Why don't you hang out of the window like other dogs?"

CROSS BRED
PUPPIES
FOR SALE

"It seemed an appropriate day to bring him along to meet them."

NICK BAKER; BANX, © 1982 PUNCH; DONEGAN, © 1985 PUNCH; HAYWARD WILLIAMS, THE SATURDAY EVENING POST; "FFOLKES' FAUNA," HARRAP LIMITED, © MICHAEL FFOLKES, 1977. GALLAGHER, "ANIMALS, ANIMALS, ANIMALS," HARPER & ROW; MIKE SCOTT; GRAHAM, "DAUGHTER IN THE HOUSE"; BOOTH, © 1983 THE NEW YORKER MAGAZINE INC

NIGHT
and the Driver

BY HERSCHEL LEIBOWITZ AND ALFRED OWENS

**Darkness spells danger when you're at the wheel.
Understanding why can save lives**

MORE than half of all road deaths occur at night, despite the fact that far fewer miles are driven then.

The reasons for this difference include the usual suspects—fatigue, drinking, reduced visibility. But a more insidious problem plays a major role in the night-time death toll: the misplaced confidence most of us have that we are able to drive safely at night as fast as during the day.

Consider the kinds of accidents

that happen after dark. Each year hundreds of pedestrian deaths occur at night. Drivers usually say that they did not see the person in time to stop. One study found that nearly a quarter of the motorists involved claimed they heard the sound of impact *before* they saw the pedestrian.

Under ideal night-time conditions—full beams on, no glare from oncoming headlights, and the pedestrian clad in white—a driver can see a pedestrian at about 300 feet. But it takes the average motorist 315 feet to stop a car that is going 70 miles an hour. Visibility drops to less than 100 feet if the person walking is in dark clothing and the driver is using dipped headlights.

This problem is compounded by the fact that people on foot consistently overestimate how well drivers can see them. To the pedestrian, it is hard to imagine being inconspicuous while bathed in intense illumination from headlights. But, in reality, pedestrians usually present very little contrast to the night roadway scene and are nearly invisible to oncoming traffic until it is too late.

Another tragic night accident is an "under-ride collision," in which the bonnet of a car slides under a larger vehicle such as an articulated lorry crossing a rural road. This illustrates how drivers run into obstacles they would never hit in daylight. In one such accident a few years ago, a young couple was driving home one clear winter evening. As they came over a small hill, a lorry-driver, about 900 feet down the road, was backing an articulated lorry into his driveway.

The car driver probably saw the lorry's headlights in the oncoming lane but not the 45-foot-long trailer extending broadside across the road. The car ploughed under the body of the trailer, tearing off the car roof and killing both occupants instantly. Only ten feet before impact did skid marks appear.

Such under-ride collisions demonstrate the need for improved lighting and other safeguards on potential obstacles.* But another important part of the problem is our misperception of the risks involved in night-time driving. And there is a neurophysiological basis for this seemingly irrational behaviour.

Visual tasks can be classified into two modes. The more familiar is the recognition mode. We use it to identify *what* we are looking at. The other is the guidance mode, which works automatically, and helps us to decide *where* objects are and to guide our movements.

The driver's primary job is steering along the path ahead, which depends mostly on the guidance mode. The motorist must also check dashboard instruments, read road signs and monitor surroundings for potential obstacles. These activities require the recognition mode. In good light, experienced drivers have little

---

*Later this year sideguards and side lamps will be made compulsory on all heavy goods vehicles.

trouble using both modes of vision at the same time.

The trouble comes when night falls. The guidance mode is not affected appreciably, but recognition functions, such as acuity, sensitivity to contrast, and the ability to perceive objects, degrade rapidly.

Since the guidance mode is not impaired, the driver can steer the vehicle as easily at night as during the day. And the most frequently used "recognition" information is artificially enhanced to compensate for the loss of daylight. Dashboard instruments are illuminated, and other vehicles normally have headlights and rear lights on.

These artificial improvements increase safety in one way, but also unjustifiably enhance motorists' self-confidence. Since road signs and instruments are easy to see, and the guidance-vision system continues to function well, drivers fail to realize that other visual-recognition tasks have become far more difficult. A driver who has not yet had a night accident is unlikely to appreciate that many of the dangers he faces are effectively invisible, that the great hazards of night driving—animals, pedestrians, cyclists, motorcyclists and vehicle breakdowns—will be seen too late.

Other conditions can also produce a dangerous discrepancy between self-confidence and ability. Alcohol, for example, enhances a driver's self-confidence while impairing judgement and reaction time. The combined effects of alcohol and diminished vision are extremely dangerous because they compound the discrepancy between ability and self-confidence.

Our roads have been getting safer for decades, but night-time fatality rates are still too high and can be reduced. An obvious step towards greater safety is improved road markings and illumination. Another might be to legislate different speed limits for day and night. This would be particularly important on secondary roads, which are likely to have cross traffic, pedestrians and other unpredictable obstacles.

But the most important step is education: teaching drivers and pedestrians about selective impairment of vision at night. Increased driver awareness of the special risks of night-time driving would make our roads much safer and help reduce fatalities.

CONDENSED FROM PSYCHOLOGY TODAY (JANUARY 1986), © 1985 THE AMERICAN PSYCHOLOGICAL ASSOCIATION, WASHINGTON, DC. BOX MATERIAL REPRINTED FROM POPULAR MECHANICS (AUGUST 1984) © 1984 THE HEARST CORP. ALL RIGHTS RESERVED. ILLUSTRATION: STEPHEN ADAMS

Caught in Passing

WIFE to spouse: "I don't want to brag, but here we are in February and I've kept every one of my New Year's resolutions. I've kept them in a manila folder in the back of my desk." — *Orben's Current Comedy*

IN THE beauty salon: "I would never have believed that story about Edna if I hadn't started it myself." — "The Girls," News Group Chicago

AT A party: "I'll say he's indecisive. The only thing he ever takes a stand on is the bathroom scales." — "Kup's Column" in Chicago *Sun-Times*

Special Effects

OPENING an exhibition of photographs at London's Royal Festival Hall, conductor André Previn said that he felt "totally out of place."

Years ago, it seems, he bought one of those tiny spy cameras, immediately shot off a whole film, and took it to the camera shop to be processed. When he went back to pick up the prints, he was called upon to give a demonstration of his photographic technique.

"You have," said the assistant, "taken 72 pictures of your eye." — "Peterborough" in *The Daily Telegraph*

I OCCASIONALLY do freelance photography for local newspapers and magazines, and take great pride in my work. At a party one evening, I was introduced to an extremely pompous gentleman who writes a weekly piece for a publication that had just used one of my pictures. After telling me how he liked the "rather interesting" composition and tones I had used in my latest work, he said, "You must have a good camera."

I then mentioned that I had enjoyed his most recent article, and added, "You must have a good typewriter." — Alexander Buiel

Buy-Lines
by Madeleine MacDonnell

Use the enquiry coupon on page 11 to get any further information. Don't miss Hints for your Home on page 16 on, and Holiday Ideas from page 169 onwards.

The rewards of plate collecting are explained in a free information pack from the **Bradford Exchange**. A subsidiary of the world's largest exchange in all major collector's plates currently traded, they'll help you discover the true beauty of plate collecting. To be valuable a plate does not necessarily have to be old and, of course, a collection of plates makes a most attractive display. In the information pack you'll find illustrations of the world's most famous hallmarks together with the prices of over 800 plates. Get your free copy by putting **66** on the coupon on page 11.

Gardeners, that fine old Lincolnshire mail order nursery **Spalding Bulb** will send you their magnificent new *Catalogue and Guide to Scent and Colour in your Garden* (usual cost 60p) free! With it you'll get details of a lawn and garden sprayer being offered free to gardeners who send qualifying orders promptly. The catalogue is packed with money-saving offers on an enormous choice of bulbs, roses, shrubs, trees, plants, hedging, fruits and climbers. For your free copy phone 0775 4436 (quote reference 50) or put **71** on the coupon.

Nutrient tablets are sometimes absorbed too quickly, so let me tell you about vitamins with a built-in time clock. **Blackmores** *Naturetime* is a 'sustained release' vitamin and mineral range. 25% of the potency of each tablet is released within an hour or so; the balance is gradually staggered over the next 8 hours giving maximum benefit. Free of sugar, yeast, milk derivatives, artificial preservatives and colours, everyone—including diabetics—can take advantage of this natural health range. For more information, put **65** on the coupon on page 11.

Does your telephone suit your lifestyle? Every taste and need is covered in the **British Telecom** telephone range. For example, the *Freeway* allows you to receive and make calls up to 100 metres from the base unit. In two-tone grey, it has push-button dialling, automatic redial of last number dialled and a secrecy button for private asides. The *Slimtel* in a choice of blue, maroon and off-white offers a whole host of up-to-the-minute features at a remarkably low price. Call British Telecom Direct, *free*, on **0800** 444 100 for a free 24 page colour catalogue. Or put **67** on the coupon.

New writers are in great demand. However, a talent for writing is not enough: there are skills and techniques to be learned. **Successful Writers** teach writing as a profession, for publication, for profit. The school provides unlimited, personal tuition via its home study course. You study at your own speed, coached by professional writers and, if your writing is not earning money by the time you have finished the course, Successful Writing will refund your fee in full. Get their free 24-page booklet, *Secrets of Successful Writing*, by putting **73** on the coupon on page 11.

Who gets the seasoned air traveller's vote? It's **South African Airways**. As well as the biggest choice of non-stop flights to and from South Africa, they offer the biggest choice of destinations all over the country. With more cabin staff to attend to your needs, extra space and better seating, superb cuisine and complimentary wine (acknowledged as the best on the route), it's not surprising that SAA get so many letters of praise. SAA also offer special discounts for car hire and hotel accommodation and a unique "See South Africa" fare. See your Travel Agent, or **70** on page 11.

'I Don't Want to Be a Mechanical Boy'

BY RENA DICTOR LeBLANC

How Peter brought the walls of his handicap tumbling down

BY THEIR son's first birthday, Jim and Barbara Van West were worried about Peter. Although he had been a healthy and alert baby, he was strangely quiet. Peter would rock back and forth on his hands and knees for hours, or stare blankly at the wall.

He was walking at 15 months, but he still didn't talk at two years old. Barbara, an attractive and dynamic woman, felt heartsick. When she gazed into her son's eyes, they would remind her of the eyes of starving children: "huge, bottomless, full of confusion."

After the Van Wests' second son, Jeffrey, was born in 1968, it became even more evident there was something terribly wrong with Peter. Jeffrey was active and responsive while his elder brother remained anchored in his silent world.

Peter was tested repeatedly. The findings indicated retardation, possibly due to hydrocephalus (increased fluid in the cranium). But no one could say for sure.

When Peter was three the couple enrolled him in the pre-school programme at a school for handicapped children in Providence, Rhode Island. At home they succeeded in teaching Peter to say about 30 half-words, like "cay" for cake. To their amazement they discovered the little boy had taught himself to read some words in his *Winnie-the-Pooh* book. Yet, at four, he still couldn't really talk, wasn't toilet trained and, worse, he was becoming more withdrawn.

One morning Barbara heard Peter scream in the kitchen. She ran in and found him standing in the corner, shrieking as though he'd seen hell. Barbara clutched him to her and sank to the floor, rocking her little boy as he screamed on and on.

When Peter's hysteria ended, Barbara sat there, with Peter still in her arms, and resolved: "This is not the way my child is going to go through life."

Someone at Peter's school recommended they get a psychological evaluation of Peter at Rhode Island's Bradley Hospital for children.

"Peter is autistic," they were told. "He should be put in an institution. It's his only hope."

In the Dark. Little is known about the cause of autism, a brain disorder characterized by a person's being unable to understand and communicate. It's sometimes as though the victims were trapped inside their own heads. It is rare for an autistic child to attend an ordinary school, much less pass examinations. Services for autistic children were just beginning to develop then, and Bradley Hospital had begun an intensive, live-in programme. It was a horrendous decision, but Jim and Barbara could come up with no other answer.

On a sunny morning in May, they took Peter to Bradley. He looked small and vulnerable in his T-shirt and jeans as his parents kissed him goodbye. Barbara hugged him one last time, then handed him to a member of staff.

Peter began to cry and stretched out his arms. They quickly turned. "It was walk away or be carried away," Barbara recalls.

Jim and Barbara were allowed to visit Peter just once a week on Saturday afternoons. Sometimes they would go to a near-by restaurant for ice-cream. They would talk to Peter and hope for some improvement or new response.

It never happened. Instead, he withdrew even further.

After almost two years, his parents asked the director of the programme for a prognosis. "Peter can stay here till he's twelve," the director told them.

"But is he going to get better?"

"I have no answer for you," was the reply.

The health insurance money which paid Peter's expenses at Bradley was running out. After much soul-searching, the couple began to look for a good hospital where he could spend the rest of his life. All hope seemed gone.

Peter's grandmother Rose, meanwhile, had journeyed to Israel. Standing beside Jerusalem's holy Western Wall, she had written a prayer on a slip of paper and pushed it into a crack. It said, "Dear God, I ask you to help my grandson."

For Peter, Bradley was an imprisonment. He slept in a high, steel hospital bed. There were strange cries of other children. He longed for the warmth of home and family.

One can never know how Peter found a chink of light in his dark abyss, but a breakthrough did occur. He was walking down a corridor at Bradley when one of the staff asked him, for the thousandth time, "Peter, what are you doing?"

Peter replied, "Talking to other people."

It was the first sentence he'd ever spoken. He was six and a half years old.

Years later he would write in a school essay: "I felt myself doomed in Bradley Hospital. I just couldn't stand it any more."

Jim and Barbara were told the news. Finally they had something to pin their hopes on. Peter had taken a giant step into the real world. One caseworker told the couple, "Get him out of here as fast as you can."

The first time Peter was brought home from Bradley, he stood wide-eyed in front of his house. His small voice was achingly uncertain as he asked, "Can go in?"

The Van Wests studied books and articles on autism. They discovered that a handful of autistic children had managed to live near-normal lives. Once the improvement started, they were helped by being treated as normally as possible. Jim and Barbara made a commitment to help Peter go as far as he could in the real world.

They enlisted the help of friends Bob and Vicki Raphael, both psychologists; they became Peter's godparents. When Peter refused to call people by name, the four adults wouldn't pay any attention to him. He learned to call them by name.

Vicki and Bob set up a therapy group in which Peter and other disabled children learned social skills.

Understanding Autism

ONE in every 2,000 children is born autistic, and some 80,000 people in the UK suffer from the condition. It occurs four times as often in boys as in girls, affecting understanding, emotion, speech and gesture. Autistic children may display ritualistic patterns of behaviour or irrational bouts of anger.

No one yet knows what causes autism. Current research is focusing on biological factors—virus infections or genetic abnormalities—that might disrupt brain development. Up to 20 per cent of sufferers undergo a sudden improvement, like Peter, at around five or six years old. But all need special care and treatment.

Further information and advice from the National Autistic Society, 276 Willesden Lane, London NW2 5RB, which celebrates its silver jubilee this year.

Jim and Barbara worked to help get a law passed in America guaranteeing every child an education, regardless of handicap. "Before the law, kids like Peter were not 'main-streamed' in school with normal children," Barbara said. "Peter was one of the first."

Teaching Peter to speak was a slow process. Abstract ideas were hard for him to grasp. He didn't recognize his feelings and had no words for them. Yet he had amazing abilities in some areas, like mathematical computation and spelling.

The Van Wests moved house in

1979, and enrolled their elder son in the local Ponaganset Middle School. Peter was placed in the special-education class of John Kelly and Vin Spremulli.

In the beginning, Kelly recalls, Peter would complain, "I can't take it. They're making fun of me." He was the child who walked with a strange side-to-side gait and kept dropping his books. He'd hardly look at anyone. His shirt might be hanging out and his nose might be running.

But there was a hunger in his eyes when he studied other children. He would sometimes imitate the way they did things. Recognizing Peter's desire to fit in, his teachers determined to help him. They showed the boy the right way to carry his books. They walked him up and down the corridor until he got it right.

Team Effort. Through the teachers' example, more and more of his class-mates became part of a remarkable support group. Some of the most popular boys and girls worked as tutors in Peter's special-education class. "The programme gave Peter some role models," Kelly says. "A lot of the kids helped him."

If Peter got a bad mark, he might yell out in class: "I don't deserve this!" But another pupil would calm him: "Don't worry. I failed the test, too." To help loosen Peter up, Kelly told him a joke each day and required the boy to tell it to five teachers. At first, Peter showed no expression. But as he saw other people laughing, he sometimes laughed himself.

Spremulli recalls, "One of Peter's strong points was that he could remember anything. So John used to play what Barbara Van West called 'Peter Games.' He'd say, 'Give me a word beginning with R that has ten letters.' And Peter would come up with a word instantly. The message spread: 'This kid's smart!'"

Peter started to progress. He was placed in an ordinary second-year class. If he was nervous he would start rocking at his desk. Teacher Mary Agnes Mason devised a signal to remind him to stop, touching him lightly on the shoulder. Eventually, Peter's class-mates took it upon themselves to give him that same gentle cue.

When Peter was 13, his family took him on an outing to the beach. It was damp and grey as evening came, and fog enshrouded them. For the moment they were an island of tranquillity.

Suddenly, Peter spoke. "I don't want to be a mechanical boy any more," he said. Autistic children do not often express their feelings, but this simple statement was wrung from his heart, heavy with resolve.

"We all cried," Barbara recalls.

Barbara and Jim and godparents Vicki and Bob organized Peter's bar mitzvah—the transition from boyhood to manhood—when he was 14. On the invitations were written the words, "We thank the Lord that we have reached this day." Peter read 23 Hebrew verses phonetically from the book of Prophets. His words were fitting. He told the story of the battle of Jericho, where the walls came tumbling down.

After the ceremony ended, Peter released balloons with labels on them telling things he wanted to let go of. "Being alone...being afraid...being different..." Trapped momentarily by a tree, the balloons were freed by a breeze that blew them away.

Peter started at Ponaganset High School, and many of the children who left the Middle School at the same time continued to keep a protective eye on him. When a pupil taunted Peter just outside school, a friend, Ken Shaw, came to Peter's rescue. He backed the boy against a wall and said, "Things like that don't happen to Peter around here!"

Peter continued to improve. As a second-year pupil he gained high marks. But during his final year Peter had a dream that seemed more difficult to fulfil. He wanted to go to the prom, the formal end-of-school dance traditional in American schools.

Finally, a blind date was arranged. Then, just a week before the big day, the girl backed out. Peter approached one of his teachers, Roland Rabitor.

"I don't know what to do," he said. "I've hired a taxi, rented a dinner-jacket and bought the tickets."

The teacher realized how important this was for him. "Let me see what I can do," he told Peter.

Rabitor consulted physical-education teacher Kathy Hazard. Kathy

A dream comes true: Peter and Brenda, king and queen of the prom

suggested Brenda Marx, a sweet, shy 19-year-old who didn't have a date either. She arranged a meeting in the gymnasium that afternoon.

Seated on a bench with the teacher between them, Peter and Brenda were achingly shy. The teacher explained, "Peter would like to take someone to the prom. And Brenda, you don't have a date. So, I thought we'd bring the two of you together. Brenda, how does that sound?"

The girl quickly replied, "That sounds great."

Kathy turned to Peter, "How about you?"

He replied, "Yes, I think that would be great."

Brenda's family couldn't afford a prom dress, so three teachers and four pupils brought their own gowns for her to choose from. The teachers clubbed together for Brenda to have her hair done.

The Quidnessett Country Club was

like an island of light overlooking the bay on prom night, April 12, 1985. From the moment Peter and Brenda entered the ballroom with its gleaming silver chandeliers, they drew delighted comments. Peter cut a dashing figure in his black dinner-jacket, and Brenda was radiant in her lavender-taffeta gown.

The boys and girls filled out ballot forms for prom king and queen during dinner, and as teachers counted the votes, two names kept cropping up. Kathy Hazard recalls, "By the time we finished, we were trying hard not to cry." The big moment arrived. First, Brenda's name was announced as prom queen. Peter walked the dazzled girl out on his arm as the crowd applauded. When the king's name was announced, "Peter Van West!" the room exploded with whoops and yells of approval.

Peter's eyes widened in disbelief under his heavy brows. "I can't believe I'm king," he said, over and over again. "I can't believe I'm king!"

The final-year class had given Peter a very special message. They were telling him they recognized the battle he'd fought to attain what most of them just took for granted—being normal.

The prom was a milestone. That night Peter fell asleep without rocking in bed. It was the first time.

Peter's school graduation ceremony in June 1985 was the realization of a dream that had sometimes seemed hopeless. To the stirring strains of "Pomp and Circumstance" played by the school band, 155 final-year pupils in their dark-green caps and gowns marched in to receive their diplomas. When the assistant headmaster announced the scholastic award, the school went wild with cheers; it was for "the senior pupil who has shown the greatest effort and determination to achieve academic success, Peter Van West."

The class went wild again when Peter walked up for his diploma.

In growing numbers, through the years, this class had reached out to help him and encourage him, and in so doing they had broadened their own humanity. Everyone knew what the head meant when he told the pupils: "This class has been helping, understanding, and has exhibited what the word love really means."

PHOTOGRAPH: BROOK BAXTER

Urning a Living

MY MOTHER, who is getting on in years, has always worked very hard, and her kindness has been a great inspiration and help to many. Recently she remarked, "There is so much to do in this world! If only one could carry on working after one has passed away, to still be of service to someone."

After a thoughtful silence, she continued, "Do you think my ashes could be made into an egg-timer?"
—Maria McNamara, Parkrand, South Africa

At One With the Eagles

BY TIM CAHILL

Is it a bird? Is it a plane? No, it's me—sky-diving

LAST year, at a dinner party, the subject of nicknames came up. I said that I'd never had one but, if the truth be told, I'd really like to be known as The Falcon. Everyone around burst out laughing.

Well, the fact is, I've been doing a little sky-diving lately, and when one learns to swoop and soar thousands of feet up in the air, then one has *earned* the right to Falconhood.

In training for a jump, the first order of business is to learn the proper touchdown technique. Our instructor,

Bill, spent an hour teaching us how to fall from a four-foot platform.

There were 12 people in the class, ranging in age from the early twenties to late thirties. One young woman was five feet tall and the least physical person in our class. The rest of us, with one notable exception, came to admire her determination. Every time Betty jumped off the platform—her face twisted into an apprehensive grimace—Pete, a cocky young petrol-station attendant, barely stifled a laugh.

Flight Plans. Next, we learned the arch: legs apart, arms outspread about shoulder level, spine bowed until you feel the strain at the small of your back. The arch, assumed upon exit from the plane, puts all the weight in the stomach, forcing the body into a horizontal position.

The classic demonstration of the efficacy of the arch is a badminton shuttlecock. Dropped with the tip down and feathers up, it falls straight to earth and is stable. The sky-diver wants that stability in the air; his arms and legs are the feathers, his stomach the tip. When the shuttlecock is turned upside-down, it flips over in its fall. A sky-diver who arches his back the wrong way, like a hissing cat, will flip over and the opening chute may come up between his legs and become entangled.

We examined the jump plane, a Cessna 182, and practised getting into the "Go" position. This involved stepping out on to the wheel and hanging from the wing strut. Betty said she wasn't sure she was strong enough to hang from the strut. Pete, who reckoned he was going to burn up the sky with his natural ability, rolled his eyes derisively. Bill said nobody should worry about hanging on to the strut. The problem, he said, was getting people to let go.

We learned that our standard, round, 28- or 35-foot canopies normally have a forward speed of about nine or five mph respectively. (More-advanced-class chutes can do about 14, and square canopies about 20.) We learned how to steer with toggles attached to directional lines, how to tell a bad chute from a good one, and what to do in the case of a water landing. Then we worked on emergency procedures.

Bill would get a student up in front of the class, strap a harness on him and yell, "Go." The student was to assume the arch position and count "Arch thousand, two thousand" on up to five thousand. The static line, attached to the parachute in our first few jumps, automatically deploys the chute in about three seconds. If, by the count of five, there is no opening shock, the main chute has malfunctioned. You must immediately pull the rip-cord on the reserve chute.

"Go."

"Arch thousand, two thousand, three . . ."

"Bam, opening shock. What do you do?"

"Check to see if it's a good chute."

"It's bad. What do you do?"

"I cut away the main chute." The

procedure is to unsnap the capewells —two hinged metal plates near each shoulder on the harness—revealing two thick wire rings. Thumbs go in the rings, you pull and the main chute goes free. Then you pull your reserve chute rip-cord.

I WAS in the second plane-load of students to jump. With me were Betty and Pete. No one spoke. The mouth was too dry, and there were too many things to think about.

Bill opened the door. The wind howled past. While I sat on the floor, he hooked me up to the static line and told me to swing my legs out—they blew towards the back of the plane with a frightening jerk. Stepping out on to the locked wheel, I grabbed the strut, then hung there, arching hard. We were 3,000 feet in the air, and everything below seemed carved in micro-miniature.

Air Force. I was supposed to look at Bill, but I don't think I did a very good job of that. He shouted, "Go!" I let go and arched. Everything happened very fast and very slow at the same time. I was supposed to shout out my arch count, but I was as silent as a stone. Those films with fellows falling off cliffs and screaming all the way down have nothing to do with reality. People have too much on their minds.

Having forgotten my count, I arched all the harder, until I could see the plane overhead. A good sign. (I had feared that as soon as I let go of the strut I'd be chopped in half by the tail of the plane. It was no use telling myself that if the plane was going at 70 mph then someone hanging from the strut was also doing 70, and would drop out of harm's way.)

I held my arch admirably, so that I was looking straight down. Then some voice shrieked in my head: *I'm falling! I'm going to end up a crimson crater in the field below.* Another voice reminded me that I had promised to hold the arch. So I compromised. I arched from the waist up. But my legs took off at a dead run.

Take-Off. Bill had told us that we'd have a tendency to run in the air. No one knows why this happens. We are frightened, certainly, and our instincts tell us to fight, or flee. Since there is nothing up there to fight, we run.

Giving in to a sprint is hilariously funny to those watching you from the plane. There I was, a second and a half out of the plane, running and dancing the fear fandango. Then, suddenly, there was a jolt on the chest strap and I was brought upright under a bright green canopy. Amid the nearest range of hills—smooth and golden, looking almost like suede—there was a great blue lake shimmering in the late afternoon sun. The sky was silent, like the inside of a vast cathedral, and I could hear the beating of my own heart.

The steering toggles were exactly where Bill said they would be and turning the chute was as easy as driving a car. I looked down through my feet to the five-acre ploughed field where I hoped to land in a small target area. A gentle breeze wafted me towards the target and I sailed with it, occasionally checking the altimeter on top of my reserve chute.

At 2,500 feet I was still above the wrong field, one with bulls in it; 2,000—I was coming in over the ploughed area; 1,800—a problem. In all that five acres there was one tree, and it was between me and the target. At 1,250 feet, I seemed to be hovering, motionless, above that damned tree.

Sinking Feeling. We had been instructed to turn our chutes into the wind at 500 feet and prepare to land. Bill had said that if there were obstacles, turn to the nearest open space. There I was, dropping out of the sky, into a tree. Jagged, upward-thrusting branches can blind you, pierce your throat. I decided *not* to land in the tree. I rode the chute to 400 until I was sure I was clear. Then I turned into the wind.

At about 200 feet the ground stopped swaying and became hugely immobile. I picked a spot on the horizon and forced myself to stare at it.

Bill had insisted that people who stare at the ground tend to do one of two things: either they stretch one foot down to the earth, like a swimmer testing the water, or they draw their knees protectively up to their chests. Both moves break legs. So I tried hard not to watch the ground, which is like trying to walk a mile with your eyes closed. Even though I

was staring at a near-by hilltop, I could see the good brown earth looming up. Then I hit the ground, rolling over on to my back in the prescribed manner.

All at once, to my utter amazement, I was up on my feet, running round the canopy so the wind wouldn't drag me across the field. I had landed only a few hundred yards from the target, on the bosom of that sweet, ploughed field.

AFTER my chute had opened, the plane banked, came back round and dropped Betty, who landed closer to the target than any of the other first-time jumpers. Pete was still up there, last one out. Betty and I waited, but we never saw his chute. By the time we got back to the hangar, the Cessna was landing. Pete wasn't on it. Bill clapped me on the back. "You ran about 50 miles before your parachute opened," he said.

"Yes," I said, "and I mucked up my count, too."

"Well, you did OK. Give yourself an 85 and remember what you did wrong."

About that time we caught sight of Pete. He was pulling his equipment over a fence a mile or so away. When he got to the hangar, he didn't seem to want to talk to anybody.

Bill was incredulous. "You wouldn't let go of the strut," he said. "That's why you landed in the back of beyond."

"OK, OK, OK," Pete said.

"You should have seen Betty," I

added, unable to resist the gibe. "She almost landed on the target."

"OK, OK, OK," said Pete. "Look, I've got to go."

IN THE next couple of weeks I jumped about a dozen more times. By my fourth static-line jump I was arching well, stable in the air and pulling a dummy rip-cord. The sixth time out I pulled my own rip-cord, and on the seventh jump I was instructed to go to a five count before opening the chute. In practice, a five-second delay plus the pull may take up to eight seconds. In that time the sky-diver reaches speeds of more than 100 miles an hour and will cover some 800 vertical feet.

The sensation becomes that of flying. It's like standing on the edge of a high diving-board. Lean out and you can feel the point at which you will fall, tumbling over in a front flip. In a free fall, from the arch position, a simple downward movement of the head accomplishes the same thing. Bring one arm in, under your body, and you'll do a complete roll.

Eventually, such acrobatics become second nature. Apart from flips and rolls, experienced divers can go into a hellishly fast headfirst dive, or modify that position to track horizontally across the sky. Starting from about 8,000 feet, on a 30-second delay, they reach terminal velocity—about 120 mph—in about 12 seconds, provided they are in the "slow" arch position.

Experienced sky-divers make a door exit—no more hanging from the strut—and can track across the sky in a fast dive towards another diver who may be in the slower arch position. At some point above his man, the tracking sky-diver will flare out into an arch, then "dock" with the first man by grabbing both his wrists. When four sky-divers do this, they form a star, and bigger stars and formations can be accomplished with 20 or more sky-divers. This is called "relative work," and is the highest expression of the sky-diver's art.

On my eighth jump the rip-cord stuck. Observers on the ground insist that they heard a loud curse boom down out of the sky, but I discount this. With no hesitation, I gave the handle a vicious two-handed yank and the main chute finally deployed.

During that jump, fear turned itself inside out and I made the important transition from falling to flying. And if, in fact, I did shout something during that flight, I prefer to think of it not as a curse, but rather as the Call of The Falcon.

Clean Sheet

TO ERR is human, to forgive is divine—but to forget it altogether is humane.

—Gloria Pitser's Secret Recipe Report

25 Ways to Look Better

BY MARY ELLEN PINKHAM

**Make the most of your health
and beauty with these quick tips**

Face Facts

Hands come in contact with more germs than do most other parts of your body. Are you in the habit of transferring these germs to your face? Break the habit and you should contract fewer colds.

Thinking of a face-lift? Lie on your back and hold a mirror above your face. Gravity will make loose skin fall back, and you will see roughly what you would look like. If the change isn't dramatic, you may want to forgo surgery and put your money in the building society instead!

Drinking six to eight glasses of water a day is good for your skin. Also, physical activity brings blood to the surface, helping to keep your skin looking great.

The Eyes Have It

Try on sun-glasses while looking in the mirror. If you can still see your eyes, and you plan to use the glasses in bright sunlight, the lenses may not be dark enough.

Watching television in the dark will *not* ruin your eyes. An American public relations man invented this notion to improve

sales for his client, a spectacle-lens salesman.

Eye-shadow will stay on better if you put the cream on first, then dust with powdered shadow of the same colour.

Footnotes

Feet sweat about one glass of water a day, so wool or cotton socks (they absorb perspiration) are the best footwear. Because they don't "breathe," synthetic socks and non-washable canvas or vinyl shoes encourage the growth of fungus.

If your back aches, check your feet. Minor foot problems such as a callus or corn and poor weight distribution can affect your walk and eventually your back.

Incorrectly fitting shoes can cause many foot complaints. Shop for shoes late in the day: your feet swell as much as half a size between morning and evening.

To refresh hot and tired feet, try soaking them in a bath with cool water.

Show of Hands

Scrape your nails over a bar of soap before you begin to work in the garden or on the car. Dirt and grime won't collect underneath.

Bleach stains off your nails by wiggling your fingertips in half a lemon, then rinsing with lukewarm water.

Hairy Situations

Don't wash that man—or that woman—right out of your hair. If you're *really* angry, you may do damage. Since hair is weakest when it's wet, it's likely to break if you tangle it up by wildly shampooing every which way. Instead, rub gently, following the line of the hair growth.

Use lukewarm water when shampooing. Very hot water will not make hair any cleaner and may burn the scalp.

To clean combs, soak them in hot water and a couple of splashes of ammonia. Scrub clean with an old toothbrush.

If your hair has too much static in it, spray your brush with one of the static-free products used for clothing.

A Mouthful

Tooth whiteners scrub away some stains, but also break down enamel—which doesn't grow back. Have regular professional cleanings instead.

Food can sometimes accumulate in the irregular surfaces of your tongue and cause bad

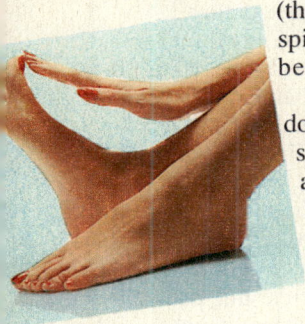

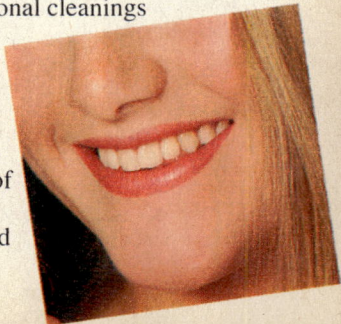

breath. Always brush your tongue when you brush your teeth.

Denture wearers should be examined every six months or so to make sure their gums are sound and their dentures still fit correctly.

Getting a Move On

Exercise isn't just for the overweight. If you don't exercise, you'll lose muscle and gain fat. Since fat is less dense than muscle is, you may not see the difference on the scales, but you will notice new bulges and bumps. Climb five more flights of stairs a day and you'll burn enough calories to lose about five pounds a year.

Few exercises improve overall health (including circulation) better than brisk walking does. Walking a mile in 12 minutes burns the same calories as jogging a mile in eight and a half minutes. There is also less chance of injury.

Love and Laughter

Men who kiss their wives before leaving for work are healthier, live longer and earn more money than those who don't.

The healthiest marriages are the ones in which partners exercise together. The least likely to succeed are those in which only the wife exercises regularly. So—play together and stay together.

If you're in the mood for romance, treat your loved one to a funny film. After being stimulated by laughter, people are more responsive to other stimuli—including the opposite sex.

A hearty laugh gives a workout to your stomach and chest muscles, heart and lungs. And though your blood pressure and adrenalin go up during laughter, they drop to normal or below afterwards, releasing stress. Laughter *is* the best medicine.

CONDENSED FROM "HOW TO BECOME A HEALTHIER, PRETTIER YOU," © 1984 MARY ELLEN PINKHAM. PUBLISHED BY DOUBLEDAY & CO, INC, NEW YORK, NY. PHOTOGRAPHS: ZEFA PICTURE LIBRARY; © SANDRA LOUSADA/SUSAN GRIGGS AGENCY

Revised Version

A YOUNG boy came home from Sunday school and proudly announced that he'd been asked to read from the Bible that morning. When asked from which book the passage had been taken, he replied, "Oh, the gossip according to John." —Douglas L. Flanders, Toronto, Canada

THE Reverend Billy Graham tells the story of the time when he arrived in a small town to preach. Wanting to post a letter, he asked a young boy where the post office was. When the boy had told him, Graham thanked him and said, "If you'll come to the church this evening, you can hear me telling everyone how to get to heaven."

"I don't think I'll be there," the boy said. "You don't even know your way to the post office." —The Methodist Recorder

Points to Ponder

I'M ALL in favour of couples living together before they get married. But only if they have to share their prenuptial bliss with a semi-trained puppy, two children with flu, and a heater that goes kerchonk all night. Under those conditions they could really get to know each other. That's what "compatible" is all about.

—Nancy Stahl, Universal Press Syndicate

PEOPLE have caught monkeys in India by setting out a small box with a tasty nut in it. There is an opening in the box large enough for the monkey to thrust in his hand, but too small for him to withdraw it once he's clutched the nut. When the monkey has grabbed the prize, he must either let go and regain his freedom or keep hold and stay trapped.

Most monkeys hold on to the nut, making it easy for hunters to pick them up. People have been known to get caught in the same kind of trap. The person who puts the goodie in the box controls the person who grabs it, but if we are willing to let go of the goodies, we are free of control.

—Elizabeth Brenner, *Winning by Letting Go*

RABBI LIONEL BLUE, on prayer:

I never started to pray because I was told to, and I never continued to pray because I ought to. I pray out of enjoyment and need. Over the years, through prayer, I have become friendly with God. You only get to friendship with any being—animal, human or divine— by talking to them and sitting with them in silence. It has taken me a lifetime to trust in these meetings. It didn't come easily.

—*Bolts from the Blue* (Hodder & Stoughton)

IF, AMONG the delights of the open world, I were to choose the sights, the sounds and the fragrances I most want to see and hear and smell on a final day on earth, I think I would choose these: the smell of pine trees in the room; the lonely calling of Canada geese; the sight of a dragonfly glinting in the sunshine; the voice of a thrush far in a darkening wood at evening; and—most spirited and moving of sights—the white cathedral of a cumulus cloud floating serenely in the blue of the sky.

—Edwin Way Teale in *Heirlooms* (Harper & Row)

POET e. e. cummings:

To be nobody-but-yourself—in a world which is doing its best, night and day, to make you everybody else— means to fight the hardest battle which any human being can fight: and never stop fighting. —"A Poet's Advice to Students," 1955

We pay £25 or more for items for "Points to Ponder." See page 1.

Cochrane RN, Devil and Liberator

BY GEORGE POLLOCK

Wronged by the Old World, he fought to free the New

Cochrane's flotilla captures the Spanish flagship "Esmeralda" at Callao, Peru, in 1820. This water-colour by C.C. Wood is in London's National Maritime Museum

WHEN a French acquaintance arrived by cab at the Mayfair home of Captain Lord Cochrane RN, begging for help, the British national hero felt sorry for him. The caller, an exile from Napoleon's France, was Random de Berenger, soldier of fortune and expert rifle instructor; Berenger in fact was wearing the green uniform of a sharpshooter. His plea that he needed to escape from creditors prompted Cochrane to lend him civilian clothes.

It was an act of kindness that changed world history. For the Frenchman was a hoaxer. It was 1814. Britain was at war with Napoleon. Unknown to Cochrane, Berenger had appeared in Dover the previous night, February 20, as if hotfoot from France, and in the scarlet uniform of a staff officer spread sensational news: Napoleon had been killed in battle, he said. Peace was certain.

Stock Exchange prices soared—and by the time the report proved bogus (it anticipated Napoleon's defeat at Waterloo by 16 months), the seven conspirators behind Berenger's charade had pulled off a massive fraud, selling stock at inflated prices.

Red-haired and six-foot-two, Cochrane, the heir to the Scottish earldom of Dundonald, was renowned for honesty as well as for dazzling courage; he gave the information that led to Berenger's arrest. However, it turned out that Cochrane made a modest profit from the affair, simply because his broker had orders to sell when stock reached a certain level.

Despite his innocence, despite his unparalleled deeds for the nation such as capturing a large enemy frigate in a brig of merely 158 tons—one of the achievements which led to Napoleon dubbing him "The Sea Wolf"—Cochrane was put on trial with the fraudsters.

He had made implacable foes in high places. As the Radical MP for Westminster he had savaged Admiralty officials for abuses like withholding seamen's pay and pensions. As a sea captain, having attacked the French fleet in the Bay of Biscay with explosive ships of his own invention—the first "torpedoes"—and driven the enemy helplessly aground, he had publicly denounced his Commander-in-Chief for failing to go in for a spectacular kill.

To ensure a "Guilty" verdict at Cochrane's trial a compliant witness was found: the cabby who drove Berenger to Cochrane's home. "I will swear black is white if I am paid for it," he boasted afterwards.

In court he swore that Berenger called on Cochrane wearing not a green uniform but the scarlet one used for the Stock Exchange hoax—perjury that caused the Lord Chief Justice, a bitter political opponent of Cochrane, to declare in outrage: "He came before Lord Cochrane blazoned in the costume of his crime!"

Cochrane was fined £1,000, gaoled for a year and expelled from both the House of Commons and the Royal Navy. His banner as Knight of the Bath, awarded after the "torpedo" ships engagement in the Bay of Biscay, was stripped from the Henry VII Chapel in Westminster Abbey.

Recognizing that the trial had been rigged, Cochrane's constituents enthusiastically voted him back to Parliament. His fine was refunded to him by public subscription. But he could not be restored to the Royal Navy. At 40, Britain's greatest seaman of his day, whose name has been ranked with those of Nelson, Drake and Rodney, was unemployed.

Blue Yonder. Abroad though, his reputation stood high. Chile, one of Spain's South American colonies, was breaking free after three centuries of despotic misrule, and in 1817 its new head of government, the improbably named General Bernardo O'Higgins, son of an Irish soldier of fortune, offered Cochrane command of the Chilean navy. Cochrane accepted, sailing off for Santiago, the Chilean capital, with his young wife Kitty and their sons Tom and baby Horace.

Chile's independence was precarious. Spain still had a garrison at Valdivia, some 450 miles south of Santiago, and a Spanish fleet of more than 40 ships dominated the Pacific; it could blockade ports at will. To deal with this threat Cochrane was given a navy consisting only of his flagship, the 50-gun ex-Spanish frigate *O'Higgins*, two worn-out former merchant ships and four small brigs. Undaunted, he set out to attack with explosives and rockets the main Pacific stronghold of Spanish power: the heavily fortified naval base of Callao in neighbouring Peru.

Cochrane's five-year-old son Tom

managed to stow away on board *O'Higgins*. As the frigate went into action at Callao a cannon-ball penetrated the ship's side and decapitated a marine, scattering his brains over Tom. "I am not hurt!" piped the tot to his horrified father.

"Put your head in the hole the shot made and stay there," Cochrane told him. "No shot will ever come through the same hole again." Tom obeyed, and survived.

The attack on Callao had the result of bottling up most of the Spanish fleet in the port. It also earned Cochrane the title of "El Diablo." He did more to justify his devilish sobriquet by setting sail for Valdivia. The garrison town, 14 miles up river from an almost land-locked harbour ringed by 15 forts, seemed impregnable. Yet as Cochrane confided to his commander of marines: "Operations unsuspected by the enemy are, when well executed, certain to succeed whatever the odds."

He landed 300 soldiers with bayonets to storm the harbour's outermost defences. The 1,000 defenders were routed, Cochrane chasing them panic-stricken from fort to fort. Survivors who escaped up river to Valdivia sacked and then abandoned the town.

Crest of a Wave. Next, on the night of November 5, 1820, Cochrane returned to Callao leading a flotilla of 14 launches carrying 240 men and made straight for the Spanish flagship *Esmeralda*. She was guarded by 27 gunboats and shore batteries of 300 guns, but in a meticulously planned 15-minute assault the capture of *Esmeralda*, her admiral and his staff was complete.

Cochrane rounded off his triumph by tracking down stray vessels, until he was able to say that in less than three years he had captured, forced to surrender or destroyed every Spanish ship in the Pacific. For Chile and Peru, independence was assured.

Up Anchor. After these successes Cochrane would have been content to retire to his Chilean estate near Valparaiso. But in 1822 an earthquake destroyed his newly completed home. He accepted an invitation to command the navy of Brazil, a Portuguese colony struggling for freedom. With six ships—soon reduced to only two capable of combat—he sailed from Rio de Janeiro, bound for the vast Brazilian northern provinces under Portugal's control.

Cochrane put about the story that he would sail into the narrow-necked bay on which Bahia (today Salvador) stood, and attack the Portuguese fleet. Predictably, the Portuguese admiral, having heard of the havoc caused by El Diablo's "torpedoes" against the French in the Bay of Biscay, ordered his fleet to sea, accompanied by 60 merchantmen.

Cochrane simply waited for the vessels to nose out into the Atlantic, then picked them off one by one. He disarmed and dismasted them, including troopships carrying thousands of soldiers to reinforce the northern provinces, and emptied their freshwater casks so that they were obliged to limp back to Bahia.

Within three years of Cochrane's arrival in Brazil, Portugal gave the colony its freedom. Remarkably, he had helped to liberate the fifth largest country in the world without a single fatality among his men.

Weather Eye. Throughout his career Cochrane's first concern was always the safety of those who served him. As Captain Frederick Marryat, the novelist, wrote in the log he kept as a midshipman under Cochrane: "I never knew anyone so careful of the lives of his ship's company, or anyone who calculated so closely the risks attending any expeditions."

This foresight contrasted sharply with the apparently outrageous chances Cochrane took. He thrived against heavy odds; delighted in not conforming to expectations.

Born at Annsfield, Lanarkshire, on December 14, 1775, Cochrane was intended for the army by his father. Instead, he joined the Royal Navy. Cochrane's Uncle Basil promised to leave him his huge fortune if he would marry an heiress of Basil's choice. Instead, a true romantic, Cochrane eloped with Kitty Barnes, a bewitchingly pretty 16-year-old orphan, 20 years his junior, who had caught his eye as she walked through Hyde Park in a school crocodile.

He was a dashing suitor—a captain who had sailed into Plymouth with three five-foot gold candlesticks, booty from the Spanish Main, lashed to his mastheads. He had won fortune for his crew and himself by capturing South American treasure ships. From a ten-week cruise his prize-money was £75,000.

By the time Spain rose against Napoleon in 1808, Cochrane was commander of the 38-gun frigate *Impérieuse* and found himself helping the Spanish freedom fighters. His daring commando-style raids—destroying roads and bridges, blowing up shore batteries, signal stations and lighthouses—held up the French advance through southern Spain.

Occupying a fort which a fellow Royal Navy captain judged to be untenable, Cochrane booby-trapped the defences by entangling chain barriers with fish-hooks, and creating a greasy slope that sent intruders hurtling into a pit. By such ploys he was able, with fewer than 200 men, to stall 1,200 French assault troops and for 15 days halt a 6,000-strong army.

Run Aground. When in 1826, having ended his Chilean and Brazilian adventures, Cochrane was asked again to fill the role of liberator and help free Greece from Turkish rule, he could not resist the challenge. But even the Sea Wolf could not turn the Greek navy into an effective force.

As always, he had a bold plan— to capture Alexandria, where Turkey's Egyptian allies had a fleet ready to embark against Greece. Two of his fire-ships sailed into Alexandria and destroyed an Egyptian man-of-war. However, when 20 other Egyptian vessels weighed anchor to flee, the Greek crews thought they were about to counter-attack. They turned their ships about and fled.

Greek independence had to wait until the sinking of the Turkish fleet at Navarino in 1827 by the combined might of Britain, France and Russia.

Turn of the Tide. Having fought his last sea battle Cochrane, now the tenth Earl of Dundonald on the death of his father, began the fight to clear his name. Kitty Dundonald, who had resolutely stood by her husband on the deck of a man-of-war in action—once even firing a ship's gun—now pleaded his case with the new monarch, William IV, the Sailor King. Cochrane was awarded a free pardon (less than he wanted, since it implied that he had been guilty of a crime) and was restored to the Navy List as a rear-admiral.

He began a campaign to get a reluctant Admiralty to accept that the age of steam had come. He could speak with authority: he had introduced the first steamship to the Pacific, developed a rotary steam-engine and designed a propeller to replace paddle wheels. His range of ideas, from smoke-screens to chemical warfare, was boundless. Cochrane's patent for using air pressure in tunnelling later made possible London's Blackwall Tunnel.

At the age of 72 Cochrane became Commander-in-Chief of the North American and West Indies stations, for the first time commanding a British fleet. Young seamen who served with him knew him as "Dad," marvelling at the unquenchable spirit of the man who had known Nelson and followed his advice: "Never mind manoeuvres—always go at them."

On the outbreak of the Crimean War, Cochrane immediately volunteered to command a naval force against Russia. Those quashing the offer of the 79-year-old admiral reported to Queen Victoria: "Age has not abated the adventurous spirit of this gallant officer, which no authority could restrain; and being uncontrollable it might lead to most unfortunate results." It could also have brought swift victory and saved many of the 35,000 French and British soldiers killed in the Crimea.

The Queen delivered her verdict on Cochrane when he died in 1860, aged 85. On the day before he was buried in Westminster Abbey she ordered that his banner as Knight of the Bath be restored to its place of honour in the Henry VII Chapel. It was more than a salute to a hero; this was acknowledgement that Thomas, Lord Cochrane had been falsely tried and wrongly convicted. It was his clear vindication.

ILLUSTRATIONS: PAGE 110, NATIONAL MARITIME MUSEUM, LONDON; PAGE 111, COURTESY OF THE EARL OF DUNDONALD

Cooking His Goose

AN ITEM on a Yorkshire restaurant menu was headed "The Chef's Special." Below it, someone had pencilled in: "Perhaps he is, but his food is awful."

—"Observer" in *Financial Times*

Picasso With Feathers

BY JARED DIAMOND

The bowerbird knows what he likes, but is it art?

MODERN animal studies have whittled away at our prejudice that human behaviour is unique. Animals engage in warfare, for instance, transmit habits culturally and even learn rudimentary languages. But does art have its animal practitioners, too? Consider the bowerbirds of New Guinea and Australia and their highly decorated bowers.

In a five-year study of bowerbirds in the remote mountains of New Guinea, I concentrated one summer on the gardener bowerbird. On Mount Wandammen, the elaborate bowers of these feathered Picassos are based on a tower of sticks nearly three feet high. This serves as the centre pole for an umbrella-shaped hut six feet across that rests on a circular mat of green moss.

On the downhill side is an entrance, with chunks of hard, black fungus facing it a few feet away. Other decorations, in

One satin bowerbird (main picture) took only blue pegs from a clothes-line offering many colours. He eventually amassed 67. Left: prize items from several bowers. Above: raiding another male's display

dazzling colours that vary from bower to bower, are piled inside the hut and on the moss mat outside: fungi, fruits and flowers, leaves and bark, butterfly wings and beetle skeletons. Even cast-off or stolen human artefacts, like matchboxes or poker chips—my own contributions —become artistic materials.

As flowers wilt and fruits rot, fresh ones are brought in. Often, decorations are grouped by colour: red fruits, leaves and flowers in one pile, orange flowers and fungus in another.

All this decorating, not unlike the proverbial etchings that men use to lure women to their lairs, is motivated by sex. Each adult male erects a bower and remains near it while the females cruise by. Only after inspecting many bowers and owners does a female choose a male, enter his bower and mate with him. Sucessful males seduce more than 30 females in a single season, but a far greater number get none.

Evidently the quality of decoration is important to the female, but why did the bowerbirds' mating system evolve along these lines? And is it really so unlike that of other birds or even our own?

The late Thomas Gilliard of the American Museum of Natural History noticed that males with the brightest plumage build the simplest

bowers. Macgregor's bowerbird, for instance, has a large, gold crest, but his stick tower is quite spartan. The male gardener bowerbird is dull brown and builds the huge and lavish bowers I saw.

Gilliard proposed that, in the course of evolution, the less resplendent bowerbird male draws female attention away from body adornment to ornaments—making himself less conspicuous to predators but no less fascinating to females.

Viewed from this perspective, bowerbirds seem rather human. Like a preening human male, the male bowerbird seeks to make the most of his visible assets. At the start of the breeding season, he works for weeks on his bower. Afterwards, he stays near it, keeping decorations fresh and guarding against raids by rivals.

Mating success depends on ownership, and the surest way to destroy a rival's sex appeal is to wreck his bower. Consequently, part of each male's day is spent visiting neighbours to steal ornaments or to tear apart their stick huts and towers.

I studied two almost identical populations of gardener bowerbirds, about 135 miles apart, and found dramatic differences of style in bower construction. For example, the birds on the Kumawa Mountains do not build huts, but erect up to five towers of sticks, each nine feet high. Beetle skeletons are the only decorations that Wandammen and Kumawa bowers share.

At first, I wondered if these

JARED DIAMOND, a professor of physiology at the University of California and a noted ornithologist, has studied the ecology of the birds of New Guinea for 20 years.

differences might be due to availability of materials, but quickly eliminated this hypothesis. Fruits, flowers and mushrooms growing close to Kumawa bowers were not used. Conversely, acorns, stones and small snail shells were available but not used on Mount Wandammen. It seems likely to me that the design typical of each area is not instinctive but learned through imitation.

Both on Mount Wandammen and in the Kumawa Mountains, I was struck by differences among neighbouring bowers. One Kumawa bird mixed brown and grey snails in the same pile; a neighbour put brown snails near the centre and grey ones near the periphery. Two birds specialized in butterflies, one in purple flowers, two others in orange fungus.

To explore these differences, I decorated bowers with numbered poker chips of seven different colours. Almost all the Kumawa birds promptly threw my decorations away. Wandammen birds, however, selected not only among my own decorations but also stole chips from neighbours.

The birds were so tame that a major problem was to stop them taking other things. One bird stole a blue matchbox and a yellow film carton. When a colleague collected the blue poker chips one bird had grown to love, it hopped on to his shoe, lifted his trouser turn-up, and tried to remove his blue socks.

Not until I watched birds using poker chips did I appreciate how

A spotted bowerbird tempts a mate with green fruits while a golden bowerbird (below) relies on moss

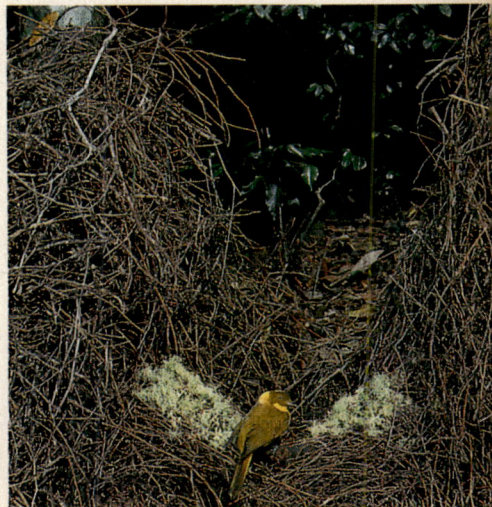

much testing went into bower decorating. One bird placed a red chip inside his hut, hopped out, went back in to fetch it again, and finally placed it next to a red leaf and red fruit just outside the entrance. Another changed his mind repeatedly about purple chips, first throwing them out, then taking them inside.

Do bowerbirds have a rudimentary aesthetic sense? Can they teach us anything about the origins of human art? Even the sober Darwin concluded that bowerbirds possess a sense of beauty. Later scientists claimed that bowerbirds are intelligent, enjoy decorating and do it as a leisure activity.

In the 1930s, an Australian ornithologist disputed these claims. He suggested that bower-building behaviour was controlled by sex hormones. Construction became simpler or even stopped when the birds were castrated. There is no proof, Marshall argued, that bowerbirds enjoy their decorations. Bower-building is simply one more hormonally controlled, goal-orientated form of behaviour with obvious sexual, social and territorial functions.

Perhaps. But I wonder. Since we can't ask the bowerbirds, how could we ever know?

Suppose a visitor from outer space came to learn whether humans had an aesthetic sense, and applied Marshall's reasoning. The visitor would attend a concert, note that the conductor, musicians and audience had a different social status, and observe signs of dominance or bonding.

A scientifically rigorous visitor who followed couples home would discover that concert-going is sometimes a prelude to sex. Castration experiments would unmask hormonal effects on concertizing males, especially on singers. Comparisons of people in different countries would reveal different musical preferences.

The visitor might well conclude: "Human concert-going superficially resembles a rudimentary form of aesthetic behaviour. However, this analogy is misleading. I obtained no evidence that humans enjoy music.

"Instead, concert-going is hormonally controlled, goal-orientated behaviour serving obvious sexual, social and territorial functions. This lowly activity does not constitute art."

So, if we view the bowerbirds as an alien from space might view us, can we be sure that human art, the highest flowering of the spirit, is still unique to man?

CONDENSED FROM DISCOVER (JUNE 1984), © 1984 TIME INC, NEW YORK. PHOTOGRAPHS: PAGES 116 AND 117, P. GREEN/N P I A W; PAGE 119, C & D FRITH/BRUCE COLEMAN LTD.

Current Comment

IF THE paper-clip were to be invented today, it would probably have seven moving parts, two batteries, three transistors and require servicing at least twice a year.
—D.A.

The Best Advice I Ever Had

BY ARTHUR GORDON

**A simple, ten-word sentence
transformed my life**

ONCE when I was facing a decision that involved considerable risk, I went to a friend much older and wiser than myself. "I'd go ahead," I said unhappily, "if I were *sure* I could succeed. But . . ."

He looked at me for a moment, then scribbled ten words on a piece of paper and pushed it across the desk. That single sentence contained the best advice I've ever had: *Be bold—and mighty forces will come to your aid*.

The words my friend had written were, I discovered later, a quotation from *The Conquest of Fear* by Basil King. They made me see clearly that when I had fallen short in the past, it was seldom because I had tried and failed. It was usually because I had let fear of failure stop me from trying at all. Fear is the most paralysing of all emotions. It can stiffen the muscles and stupefy the mind and the will.

On the other hand, whenever I *had* plunged into deep water, impelled by a flash of courage or just plain pushed by the rude hand of circumstance, I had always been able to swim until I got my feet on the ground again.

Be bold—that is no exhortation to be reckless or foolhardy. Boldness means a deliberate decision, from time to time, to bite off more than you are sure you can chew. And there is nothing mysterious about the mighty forces referred to. They are the latent powers that all of us possess: energy, skill, sound judgement, creative ideas—yes, even physical strength and endurance in far greater measure than most of us realize.

In other words, boldness can create a state of emergency to which the organism responds. I once heard a famous mountaineer say that occasionally a climber will get himself into a position where he can't back down; he can only go up. He added that sometimes he put himself into such a spot on purpose. "When there's nowhere to go but up," he said, "you jolly well go up!"

The same principle works just as surely in something as commonplace as accepting the chairmanship of a local committee or seeking a more responsible job. In either case, you know you'll have to deliver—or else. And, unless you're hopelessly unqualified, you *will* deliver. Your pride, competitive instinct and sense of obligation will see to it that you *do*.

Those particular mighty forces are, admittedly, spiritual ones. But they are more important than physical ones. While it was a hurtling pebble's centrifugal force that killed Goliath, it was courage that enabled David to face the Philistine giant in the first place.

It's curious how spiritual forces often have their counterparts in the physical world. A university friend of mine was a crack rugby player, noted particularly for his fierce tackling even though he weighed much less than the average player. Someone expressed surprise that he didn't get hurt. "Well," he said, "it goes back to something I discovered when I was a timid youngster. In one game I suddenly found myself confronting the opposing full-back, who had nothing but me between him and our goal line. He looked absolutely gigantic! I was so frightened that I closed my eyes and hurled myself at him like a panicky bullet—and stopped him cold. I learned that the harder you tackle a big player, the less likely you are to be hurt. The reason is simple: momentum equals weight times velocity."

So if you are bold enough, even the laws of motion will come to your aid.

This trait—a willingness to extend yourself to the utmost—is not one that can be acquired overnight. But it can be taught to children and developed in adults. Confidence is a cumulative thing.

To be sure, there will be set-backs and disappointments in any programme of expanded living; boldness in itself is no guarantee of success. But the person who tries to do something and fails is a lot better off than the person who tries to do nothing and succeeds.

Bold self-confidence and decisiveness often mark leaders in the business world. The most successful executive I ever worked for was a man who made almost instantaneous decisions. "At least," he used to say wryly, "I make my mistakes quickly." On one occasion someone asked this man if he didn't believe in the adage "Look before you leap."

"No," he said cheerfully. "The trouble with that axiom is if you look too long, or too often, you never leap at all."

Some people claim that our modern-day preoccupation with security is weakening our willingness to take chances. Initiative, they say, is the instinctive response to the lack of material comfort.

I disagree; people, I believe, will always seek new and more challenging worlds to conquer.

When I was a boy a man visited our class and was invited to say a few words. I don't remember who he was, but I've never forgotten what he said: "Love life. Be grateful for it always. And show your gratitude by not shying away from its challenges.

"Always try to live a little bit beyond your capacities—and you'll find your capacities are greater than you ever dreamed."

CONDENSED FROM GUIDEPOSTS (OCTOBER 1985), © 1985 GUIDEPOSTS ASSOCIATES INC, CARMEL, NY

Cold Climes

HUMORIST Keith Waterhouse has compiled a tongue-in-cheek list of amazing things you didn't know about winter. Here is a selection:

• Strong medical evidence suggests that the common cold is caused by self-pity. Research among nearly 6,000 sufferers revealed the single common factor that they all felt extremely sorry for themselves.

• The expression "Brrr!" as a comment on the cold weather is peculiar to the British. The French, for example, exclaim "Bwww!" and the Japanese "Blll!"

• Double glazing was invented by the Earl of Sandwich who, feeling a draught down his neck while at the gaming tables, instructed a servant to get some warm air and put it between two sheets of glass.

• Why is ice slippery? Scientists are not sure, but the answer is probably that the water from which ice is formed is itself slippery, in order to help it move easily when finding its own level, running out of taps etc.

• The reason so few Roman buildings survive in Britain is that most of them were constructed of packed snow. Arriving in the long hard winter of 55 BC, Caesar's troops had never seen snow before and mistook it for a local mineral. The melting of the St Alban's Coliseum in 54 BC led to terrible reprisals on the indigenous population, who were lined up and snowballed.

• Two Eskimos, frost-welded to one another while traditionally rubbing noses in sub-zero temperatures, were hired as Siamese twins by Phineas Barnum, who happened to be in Alaska at the time. Their contract was cancelled when the circus reached Southern California.

• Countrymen have a saying: Frost in December, snow in January. Frost in January, 24-Hour Emergency Plumber in February.   —*Punch*

Mandy was 9 when she was diagnosed as suffering from Friedreich's Ataxia.

Now she's 14, and crippled. Her life expectancy has been cruelly shortened. But she's brave. She's come to terms with it.

What she finds more difficult to come to terms with is the thought that her little brother Christopher might develop it too. Because Friedreich's Ataxia is a genetic disease.

So if one child develops it, there's a chance the younger one will too. At about the same age.

All the money in the world isn't going to save Mandy.

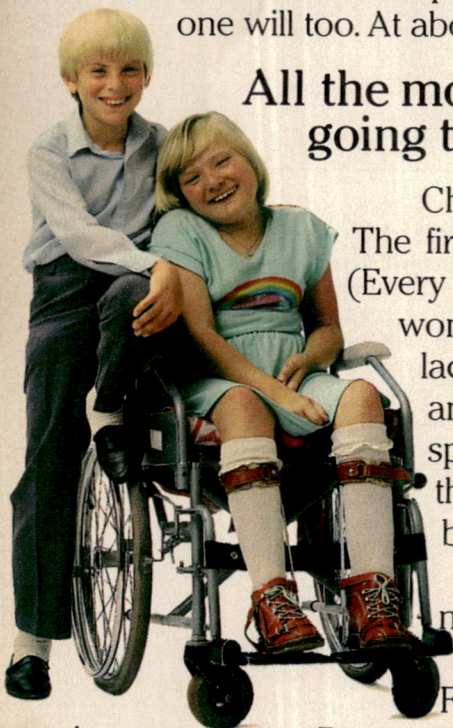

Christopher will be 9 soon. The first symptoms are unsteadiness. (Every time Chris stumbles, his parents wonder if this is the first sign.) Then lack of coordination, limb tremors and eventually, curvature of the spine sets in. The brain stays healthy, but in an increasingly useless body.

So far there is no cure. And no one has ever recovered from it.

And no one will unless the Friedreich's Ataxia Group receive your money. Because they are the only people funding research into this vicious disease in this country.

So without your donations, research will stop.

Dead.

Mandy would find that desperately hard to come to terms with.

But it might just save her little brother.

Please accept this donation to the work of the Group.

Name_____

Address_____

_____

_____

_____

_____

*I require/do not require a receipt. Please tick ___ if you require further information ___ if you would like details of Deeds of Covenant.
Send to: Hon Treasurer, THE FRIEDREICH'S ATAXIA GROUP, Burleigh Lodge, Knowle Lane, Cranleigh, Surrey GU6 8RD. Tel: (0483) 272741.

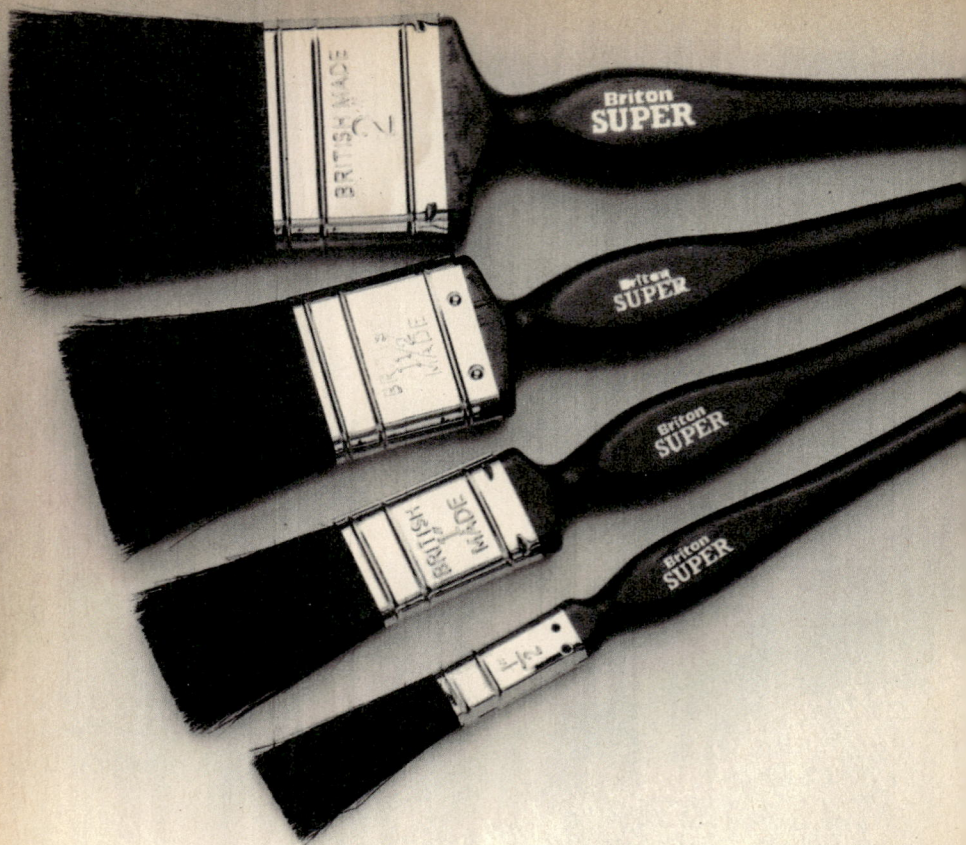

FOUR SUPER PAINT BRUSHES

Four paintbrushes to fill every painting need around your home. British-made by Briton Chadwick, this Super set of a ½", 1", 1½" and 2" brush, each with pure black bristle set in a plastic handle. Terrific value!

only **£4.50** including p&p.

To order write your name, address and "Paintbrushes" on a piece of paper, attach a cheque/PO payable to Reader's Digest and post in an envelope addressed to:
Buy-Lines, 25 Berkeley Square, London W1X 6AB.

Despatch will be prompt (usually by return) but please allow 28 days for delivery.

Reg No 340452 England

the bucket and emptied it into his basin, he thought, *Those idiots thought they could fool me with that old trick!*

It was then he realized that "those idiots" had removed the drain-pipe beneath the basin.

—Daniel Pierre

MY HUSBAND, an engineering student, often seemed to be speaking a different language when he talked about his studies. So I was amused to find that his mechanics textbook defined a "couple" as "what is formed when two forces are equal, opposite and parallel."

—Debbie Holmes

AS A "fresher" at Edinburgh University, I was taught by an elderly professor who had a good technique for silencing an audience at the start of a lecture. He simply began to move his lips inaudibly and, as students strained to hear what he was saying, a completely attentive silence would descend. He would then raise his voice to a normal level, leaving us wondering what whispered gems of wisdom we had missed.

One morning, a leg injury forced me to sit in the normally vacant front row. As the usual hubbub subsided, I caught the last few words of his scarcely audible whisper: "Rhubarb, rhubarb, rhubarb . . . " —Doreen Wilson, Kirkliston, Lothian

THE value of positive thinking was emphasized in one of my daughter's courses. For an essay assignment, she chose to review a book called *Think Yourself Thin*. Browsing through it one day, I discovered her bookmark—a neatly flattened, empty sweet wrapper.

—Fran Hill

College Rags

I WAS spending my second year of university in Paris, where the highlight of my curriculum was a phonetics course that promised to impart a true French accent. A few months later, as I was walking in my neighbourhood, a Frenchman stopped me to ask if there was a bakery around the corner.

"*Oui*," I responded, and was totally destroyed when he exclaimed, "Oh, you speak *English*!" —Robert Leb

THE favourite sport in our college hall of residence was water fights—dousing one another with water from glasses, water-pistols, balloons, even wastepaper bins. Since each room had a basin, there was endless ammunition.

The most frequent target was the resident tutor. Approaching his room one afternoon, he noticed his door was ajar. Looking up, he saw a bucket of water balanced on the door's edge ready to fall on him. As he took down

£100 is offered for your "College Rags" anecdote. Details are on page 1.

*Copy of the missing Just Judges
in Ghent's cathedral*

Mystery of the Just Judges

BY PAUL MONTGOMERY

**Searchers remain obsessed
by the most baffling art theft
of the century**

IN THE pre-dawn darkness the first
tram bell echoes down the winding
cobble-stone streets. Mist rises from
the turbid canals as the ancient Belgian city of Ghent wakes to another
day. Soon the city's medieval centre
will be crowded with visitors who come
to see its treasures: the Castle of the
Counts of Flanders, the gabled quarters
of the old merchant guilds, the vast
Cathedral of St Bavon.

It is the cathedral that is the most
intriguing, for in one of its chapels
reposes a priceless masterpiece—the
Holy Lamb altar-piece of Hubert and
Jan Van Eyck. Ever since its 24 ex-
quisitely painted panels were installed
in 1432, the altar-piece has attracted
pilgrims from around the world. Only
the most sharp-eyed of tourists would
notice that the bottom left-hand panel
lacks the glow of the rest—until
the guides identify it as a copy—a
reminder of one of the twentieth century's most sensational art thefts.

The case began on the morning of

April 11, 1934, when an under-sexton found a side door of St Bavon's unbolted. A search revealed that two of the altar-piece's paintings, each measuring 20-by-57 inches and set in the same frame back-to-back to form part of a folding shutter, had been prised loose and removed.

One, painted in the black-and-white technique known as grisaille, depicted Saint John the Baptist. The other, in the unparalleled luminous colour and meticulous detail of the Brothers Van Eyck, showed a group of horsemen, known as the Just Judges, riding through a rocky landscape towards the Holy Lamb of the central panel.

By 9am police were on the scene taking statements, and by noon a special watch had been placed along Belgium's borders and at its ports. But in those law-abiding days, Belgian police had little experience in dealing with major crimes. Crowds thronged the cathedral as news of the theft spread, and potential clues were obliterated.

To the Belgian people, the altar-piece was an enduring wonder, its details as familiar as the face of a relative; to art historians, it ranked with the *Mona Lisa* and the Sistine Chapel ceiling. Each day crowds gathered in the cathedral to hear the latest news. Some later remembered a frequent visitor, a plump man of average height, in his fifties. He was always soberly dressed, had a moustache and a gold pince-nez.

Although no one knew it then, the next important event came on April 28 when a man hired a Royal typewriter from an office-equipment shop in

The recovered painting of Saint John the Baptist

Ghent. He filled out the hire form in the name of Van Damme, but since his deposit more than covered the typewriter's value, he was not asked for identification. He was in his fifties, soberly dressed, with a moustache and a gold pince-nez.

Three days later, a letter postmarked April 30, typewritten in French, arrived at the residence of Bishop Honoré Coppieters of Ghent. "Your Excellency," it began, "We have the two Van Eyck panels. The hiding-place of the more valuable of the two is known to only one person. Any delay in replying will increase the danger of their deterioration."

The letter stated that the panels would be returned on payment of one million Belgian francs (then worth almost £7,000, and nearly eight times that today). The bishop was instructed to reply in the classified ads of *La Dernière Heure*, a Brussels newspaper. The message was signed "D.U.A."

Damaging Threat. Consultations with government officials followed, and on May 14 this advertisement appeared in *La Dernière Heure*: "D.U.A. Proposal exaggerated." Five days later "D.U.A." replied, warning that if the bishop continued stalling he would receive cut-up pieces of the Saint John panel in the post.

The worried bishop then replied that conditions were accepted, and on May 28 an envelope in the now-familiar typeface arrived, enclosing a claim ticket for luggage held at the

North Station in Brussels. Half-expecting a hoax, the police handed in the ticket at the station and received a package wrapped in brown paper. Underneath an oilcloth was the unharmed panel of Saint John the Baptist!

"Who checked this in?" the police demanded. "I don't know," the attendant answered. "He was soberly dressed, in his fifties, with a moustache." Thus, some six weeks after the crime, the authorities had one of the two panels and a description of the suspect.

On May 31 "D.U.A." sent instructions for the final exchange. The agreed ransom was to be sent to Pastor Meulepas in Antwerp, who in turn was to give it to the bearer of a torn piece of newspaper matching one enclosed in "D.U.A.'s" letter.

Ten days later, a package containing just 25,000 francs was delivered to Pastor Meulepas. With it was a letter stating that only 225,000 francs, no more, would be forthcoming. The case would be dropped if the panel was returned on payment.

The exchange took place at Pastor Meulepas's rectory on the afternoon of June 14. The bearer of the torn newspaper was a taxi-driver—the pastor's maid took down the number of the taxi before it drove away. The driver turned out to be Frans Compeers, who had been suspected of committing a number of petty crimes. He insisted he had been given the newspaper and instructed to pick up a package at the rectory by a passenger in his taxi. The man was of average height, in his fifties, soberly dressed, with a moustache and a gold pince-nez.

For the next four months, police shadowed Compeers but could find nothing incriminating. The ransom banknotes, whose serial numbers had been recorded, never surfaced. The authorities concluded that the taxi-driver, like the pastor, was an innocent go-between.

Meanwhile the bishop's reduced payment terms produced a spate of alternately pleading and threatening letters from "D.U.A."—13 in all, the last postmarked October 1, 1934. For nearly two months, the case was quiet. Then, on November 25, the investigation was turned upside-down.

At a political rally in Dendermonde, 19 miles east of Ghent, a series of speakers from the towns of East Flanders took the podium. One was a plump, soberly dressed 57-year-old stockbroker, wearing a moustache and a gold pince-nez.

His name was Arseen Goedertier, and his home and office were in near-by Wetteren. He had been a teacher of architectural drawing and a church sexton before turning to finance. His hobbies included painting and reading thrillers. He was also in deep financial trouble. A company he had founded in 1928 had just declared bankruptcy.

Following a fiery speech on solving the world economic crisis,

Scene of the crime: St Bavon cathedral

Goedertier stepped from the podium and, clutching his heart, fell to the floor. A doctor examined him at a near-by house and advised his family to prepare for the end. Goedertier summoned his trusted lawyer, Joris De Vos, to whom he gasped his last words: "I'm the only one who knows where the Holy Lamb is. The file is in the right-hand drawer of my desk under the heading 'Insurance.'" Before he could say more, Goedertier died.

After the funeral, De Vos visited Goedertier's widow. In the "Insurance" file he found copies of all the "D.U.A." letters to the bishop, cuttings of the classified ads from *La Dernière Heure*, crude sketches of a staircase and a cupboard, a claim ticket from a railway station in Ghent, and a handwritten four-page draft of a letter.

The claim ticket turned out to be for the Royal typewriter that had typed the letters to the bishop. The sketches have never been convincingly interpreted. But a sentence in the draft of the unsent letter to the bishop has intrigued searchers ever since: "The [Just Judges] panel lies in a place where neither I nor anyone else can remove it without arousing the attention of the public."

De Vos did not go to the police. To maintain the respectability of the Goedertier name, he instead consulted a noted Dendermonde judge, who conducted his own investigation, searching Goedertier's house, the church where he had been sexton, the school of architecture where he had taught. There was no trace of the panel.

Hitler's Hunter. Years passed; the case grew more distant. It was not until 1942, after German armies occupied Belgium, that interest revived, instigated by the Nazis' keen interest in what they considered to be "Aryan" art. They seized the Holy Lamb altar-piece, and set out to find the missing Just Judges panel. The case was assigned to First Lieutenant Henry Koehn, a meticulous researcher attached to the "Art Protection" unit in Brussels.

Koehn conducted interviews with Goedertier's widow, the attorney De Vos and the other surviving witnesses to the stockbroker's last days. He even had Goedertier's grave opened. Although unsuccessful, he concluded that Goedertier was not the actual thief but only a negotiator. He also believed the panel was still hidden in or near St Bavon cathedral. Meanwhile, one by one, the surviving witnesses in the case died—De Vos and Madame Goedertier in 1942. Finally, Koehn was transferred to Eastern Europe in 1943 and took his files with him.

Since the war, Karel Mortier, the Ghent chief of police, has been primarily responsible for keeping the Just Judges case alive. Together with local journalist Noël Kerckhaert, he wrote a book about the case. Through German Army archives the two traced Koehn to a remote island in northern Germany.

It was a windy day when Kerckhaert made his way to Koehn's rural cottage. His spirits fell when Frau Koehn told him that the ex-lieutenant had died the year before. But when he mentioned the Just Judges the widow said, "Yes, my husband always said that was an important matter" and led him to a room. There before him were photocopies of the Ghent police dossier as well as the lieutenant's own notes and reports.

After analysing the new documents, Kerckhaert and Mortier concluded that it would have been extremely difficult for a middle-aged man of ordinary strength working alone to extricate the heavy oak panels from the frame. They are further convinced that the art-loving Goedertier would never have destroyed the Just Judges or hidden it in a place where rot or insects could have attacked it. They believe that Goedertier, working with an accomplice, hid the Just Judges in St Bavon cathedral itself.

"A tantalizing clue," says Kerckhaert, "is that one of Goedertier's favourite tales was Edgar Allan Poe's 'The Purloined Letter,' a story that maintains the best hiding-place is out in the open." But Mortier now thinks that the panel may have been removed from the cathedral during the war and hidden elsewhere.

Kerckhaert and Mortier are not the only ones on the trail of the Just Judges. For the past 20 years, Ghent computer technician Lucien Huyghe has been making a list of buildings in and around the city that were under construction in 1934, on the theory that Goedertier's interest in architecture might have led him to use one as a hiding-place. He has searched a house near St Bavon and a chapel in a near-by town.

In October 1984 Huyghe persuaded authorities to open a war memorial completed in 1934. Like the other places, it was empty. He now seeks backing for ultrasound equipment that would allow him to look into walls without damaging them.

The file on the Just Judges remains open, and the Ghent court still gets half a dozen letters a year from people with an idea where the panel is. Anyone who has come into contact with the case cannot help but take an interest. You walk along the cobble-stone streets of Ghent's Old Town on a misty morning and hear a muffled footstep. You think of a portly man with a moustache and a gold pince-nez.

Where is the final, vital clue? Until the Just Judges panel is returned in glory to its rightful place in St Bavon, the search will go on.

PHOTOGRAPHS: GIRAUDON, PARIS; PAGE 131, ROUSSEAU/TRAVEL PICTURES

Caught Shorts

LEO BUSCAGLIA, author of *Living, Loving and Learning*, on the moment he'd most like to forget:

When speaking in public I perspire profusely, and always carry a few neatly pressed white handkerchiefs.

Once, before a large audience, I had already used two handkerchiefs. I reached for number three and proceeded to wipe my forehead—only to find to my horror that I was using a pair of pressed white briefs that had been piled among the handkerchiefs. With as much poise as I could muster, I completed the dabbing and quickly returned the underwear to my pocket.

I often wonder how many viewers in the national audience shared the "brief" embarrassment. —*Robert Morley's First Book of Bricks* (Weidenfeld and Nicolson)

There's Money in a Business at Home

BY LIZ HODGKINSON

How you can set up a thriving enterprise

IN ORMSKIRK, Lancashire, Susan Forbes runs an antiques business from her home. She sells pieces displayed in her sitting-room and undertakes commissions to find anything from just one desired item to furnishings for a whole house. Says Susan, "Running a business like mine from home doesn't require capital for premises; I have a roof over my head, I don't spend time travelling to work and, most importantly, I am my own boss."

● In Ealing, west London, Gerard and Frances Gosler's kitchen is filled with celebration cakes in various stages of completion. Every week, Frances's Cake Artistry company sells several christening- or wedding-cakes, priced from £35

Profit-makers: cake artist Frances Gosler; Finn and Anne Kennedy of Clothkits; Sylvia Longstaff and her leisure venture

to £200, some decorated by her husband, a semi-retired salesman. A self-taught specialist in the art of modelling with icing, Frances started making cakes as a hobby. "When they began to sell, I read books and went on some courses, and set up properly," explains Frances, a former shorthand typist. "I couldn't go back to working in an office."

● In the Avon village of Timsbury, Mary Holbrook spends her time looking after her herd of 90 goats, and turning their milk into specialized cheeses. She has been keeping goats for ten years and now makes up to 700 pounds of cheese a week which she sells mainly to specialist cheese shops.

This is a tiny sampling of one of the fastest-growing areas of the British economy—small businesses based at home. With conventional jobs hard to get, people are seeking new ways of working. According to the Department of Employment, more than 2·6 million Britons are now self-employed. The National Federation of Self-Employed and Small Businesses estimates that at least three out of four home-based businesses are sole proprietorships, and that annual turnovers of between £20,000 and £50,000 are not uncommon.

While the details of getting started are different for each business, people now in the field agree on six rules for success:

1. Choose work you like and can do well. There are two ways of deciding what would be right for you: either turning a hobby or activity you enjoy into a business, or looking to fill a gap in the market by providing a service that did not previously exist.

Bob Ridges, of Farrington Gurney, near Bristol, was a master mariner for more than 30 years, and gave it up to establish a business as a maker of decoy ducks. Bob became interested in carving decoy ducks as a hobby when he was at sea, but began his business with no previous experience of marketing crafts. However, he soon made his first sale by putting displays in the windows of local building societies, and people began beating a path to his door.

Today his customers come from as far away as Iceland and Israel to pay up to £1,500 for a Ridges duck. His Decoy Art Studio runs five-day courses, produces a quarterly magazine and has five employees. Now 54, Bob has been running his business for three years and has "always been able to pay the bills."

In 1983 Sylvia Longstaff was about to take an executive position with the Sue Ryder Foundation when she fell in love with a picturesque six-bedroomed house in the Yorkshire Dales. Sylvia, then 48 and widowed for 16 years, thought it would make an ideal location for holidays for people who, like herself, were single and no longer young. She rented the house furnished and put together a holiday package, advertising in the newsletter of an organization for single people where she found a ready market.

"I booked the place for a fortnight and had 12 people on each week," says Sylvia. "I found out where all the trekking centres were, hired a minibus, and booked up local restaurants for evening meals. Everyone had a marvellous time and clamoured to come back."

She booked the house for 20 weeks, and set up Longstaff Leisure as a holiday business with a difference. "I realized there was a gap in the market. There are plenty of holidays for the young and elderly, but nothing for people like myself, singles in the middle age groups."

Sylvia's House Party Holidays for singles offer a complete package of hosted walks, evening entertainment, pub games, folk nights, saunas and cycling. Sylvia does most of the catering herself and now has a team of eight helpers.

2. Organize yourself. In a home business there's nobody to tell you when to work, what to do or how to do it. But unless you have iron self-discipline, and can sort out priorities, you can get into trouble.

Some years ago, Debbie Sabine of Richmond, Surrey, was combining an office job as a computer specialist with running a home and looking after her two pre-school children. When her mother came to live with the family, Debbie thought that, as a disciplined, well-organized operator, it would be easy to carry on her work from her home as a freelance.

She set herself up as a consultant and a link between clients and computer programmers. After all, her husband was out at work all day and her mother was on hand to look after the children. But at first it just didn't work out like that.

"My mother would keep interrupting me with questions about the children's lunch," Debbie recalls. "As each piece of my work involved about 17 different logical steps, once I was interrupted, the whole thing went and I would have to start from scratch." Because she was working in one corner of the living-room, she couldn't escape the distractions.

"I soon decided that I had to have a proper office, so I converted a bedroom and put in a separate telephone line. Now, when I'm 'in the office,' nobody is allowed to interrupt me and I'm completely professional."

3. Get to know the laws and regulations covering home business. There are no specific prohibitions on operating from home, though you will need planning permission from the local authority if you have to make major structural alterations, or substantially change the use of the house—to run it as a shop, for example.

Make sure you are not causing traffic congestion, or causing a nuisance to the neighbours. It makes sense to install sound-proofing if your business is noisy, and ensure that visitors do not block entrances used by others.

Notify your building society if you

are a house owner—some mortgage contracts prohibit you from using your home for business purposes. If you are in rented accommodation, make sure that your landlord has no objection.

It is essential to arrange proper insurance cover. A domestic policy will not cover business equipment and stock, or accidents to business visitors who call at your home. Even domestic claims could be invalid if you do not notify your existing insurance company of your business plans.

It is also important to know the tax rules. The profits of a business, after deduction of expenses, are taxable. If you use one or more rooms of your house exclusively for your business, you will be able to claim a proportion of rent, rates, telephone, heating, lighting and insurance as bona fide business expenses. On the other hand, if you claim tax relief for these expenses, you may be liable for capital gains tax on part of any profit you make from subsequently selling your house.

Look into VAT regulations. If your turnover exceeds, or looks likely to exceed, £20,500, you must notify your local VAT office and may well be required to register. Below that limit, registration is voluntary, but might be to your advantage, since it allows you to claim back VAT you have paid on incoming supplies.

4. Use your mind instead of your money. The most important factor in making a home venture possible, and eventually a success, is the opportunity to operate on a shoe-string by combining work and residence. "If you have a problem," one home-business operator stresses, "don't throw money at it. Throw your mind, your energy—your spirit."

5. Get help and advice. An estimated 75 per cent of home businesses are one-man shows. But going it entirely alone can be costly. You may need to consult professionals—an accountant for advice on tax and record-keeping, an insurance broker to ensure that you are properly protected and, if you decide to form a partnership or a limited company, a lawyer.

A wide range of advice and support is on offer. The Enterprise Allowance Scheme, started in 1983, has already provided more than 120,000 would-be entrepreneurs with initial funding. Some 240 local enterprise agencies throughout the country give free commercial counselling to anyone planning to start their own business. Local DHSS offices have leaflets available on National Insurance contributions, and Inland Revenue offices on tax, for the self-employed.

A home business can often benefit from outside help. Honeychurch Toys, established by Gil Honeychurch and her husband in Market Lavington, Wiltshire, ran successfully as a husband and wife enterprise until Gil's husband died, leaving her with the dilemma of either going it

Next time you catch cold, drop in on your pharmacist.

All sorts of ailments can give you symptoms of a cold.

Your pharmacist is familiar with them.

If your cold is of the common variety, he can give you help and advice on the spot.

If, however, he suspects you have something uncommon, he will, of course, pack you off to your G.P.

Who, in turn, may send you back to your pharmacist with a prescription.

Your doctor and pharmacist make a good team.

Especially if you know how to use them properly.

Ask your pharmacist. You'll be taking good advice.

alone, or closing down the business. Instead she took on a partner.

Says Gil, "My husband and I were content to run the business on a small scale. My partner is a trained designer, full of ideas—and with his own family to support. Since he joined we have taken up all the Government's free enterprise offers, we employ three full-time youngsters, and we've quadrupled our output."

6. *Know your personal "bottom line."* Sooner or later, successful home-business people must decide whether they're seeking expansion beyond the home, with its prospects for greater profit, or the independence of staying by the fireside.

Consider Clothkits, a mail-order clothing firm which was started in the home of Finn and Anne Kennedy in Lewes, East Sussex. They have built up a business with a £6 million annual turnover, and employ about 240 people, mostly locals who work either from *their* homes or in a cheerful workshop behind a Victorian shop-front in Lewes High Street.

"When we had to expand," says Finn, "we made a decision to keep to the essential cottagey, home-based type of business we had begun. So we have expanded only locally,

rather than go for the big time with factories on industrial trading estates. After all, we started Clothkits for fun; that and the satisfaction of personal involvement at every level is the point of having a home business."

There are many books available which cover starting and running a business from home. Among the most useful are: "Earning Money at Home," edited by Edith Rudinger and published by the Consumers' Association; "The Small Business Guide," by Colin Barrow, BBC Publications; "Working for Yourself: The Daily Telegraph Guide to Self-Employment," by Godfrey Golzen, published by Kogan Page.

For free advice on setting up a small business, dial 100 and ask for Freefone Enterprise. Other sources of information are: National Federation of Self-Employed and Small Businesses Ltd, 140 Lower Marsh, Westminster Bridge, London SE1 7AE; local enterprise agencies (look in the telephone directory, or consult your town hall or Citizen's Advice Bureau); The Council for Small Industries in Rural Areas (CoSIRA), 141 Castle Street, Salisbury, Wiltshire SP1 3TP.

PHOTOGRAPHS: PAGE 134 AND 135 (TOP), MICHAEL TAYLOR; PAGE 135 (BOTTOM) ROGER SCRUTON

To Whit?

THE eleventh Duke of Norfolk is fondly remembered for the tame owls which he bred in the keep at Arundel Castle, naming them after prominent friends. One morning at breakfast a footman announced: "Your Grace, I have to inform you that Lord Thurlow has laid an egg."

—"PHS" in *The Times*

SECRET EXODUS
The Story of Operation Moses

BY CLAIRE SAFRAN

From "Secret Exodus: The Story of Operation Moses"
to be published by Prentice Hall

SECRET EXODUS
The Story of Operation Moses

"In that day a great trumpet will be blown, and those who were lost in the land of Assyria and those who were driven out to the land of Egypt will come and worship the Lord on the holy mountain at Jerusalem." Isaiah 27:13

For more than 2,000 years the black Jews of Ethiopia, descendants of one of the lost tribes of Israel, preserved their heritage and their stubborn belief in the Old Testament prophecy that one day they would return to Jerusalem. In the 1970s, after a Marxist government assumed power in Ethiopia and began to oppress religious minorities, the Jews were more determined than ever to leave. But emigration was barred, and the unofficial way out was paved with peril.

Then, in the spring of 1984, Israel and the United States put together a covert plan—Operation Moses—to airlift these forgotten people to Israel. The story of that daring rescue effort can now be told.

ETHIOPIA sits behind a fortress of craggy mountains in north-eastern Africa. For centuries in the northern provinces of Gonder and Tigray there lived a people known as *falashas*, a word meaning strangers or exiles in Amharic, the modern Ethiopian language. They called themselves Beta Israel, the House of Israel, the lost tribe of black Jews of Ethiopia.

Early in 1984, something extraordinary happened in the falasha villages, scattered like chaff among the farm lands of the Lake T'ana region, or perched among the peaks of the Simēn Mountains. The miracle began with a message delivered to hundreds of primitive hamlets. Some say the word to leave came as a quick whisper in a dusty market-place. Others heard it from swift messengers coming and going like night shadows along the narrow roads.

The news they carried meant the fulfilment of Isaiah's Old Testament prophecy of their deliverance. "We come from Jerusalem," the elders had said for more than 2,000 years. "One

CONDENSED FROM "SECRET EXODUS: THE STORY OF OPERATION MOSES," © 1986 CLAIRE SAFRAN. THE BOOK WILL BE PUBLISHED IN AUTUMN 1987 BY PRENTICE HALL PRESS, NEW YORK, NY. PHOTOGRAPHS: SVEN NACKSTRAND/FRANK SPOONER PICTURES; © JOHN HILLELSON AGENCY; M. BARAM/JOHN HILLELSON AGENCY; CASTELNUOVO/REX FEATURES LTD day we will return to Jerusalem."

Over the years, from each village, a few had left, walking north-west by night across the dangerous miles to the Sudan, where they languished in refugee camps. Now, the messengers said, many had been taken to Jerusalem. And the ones who followed would be too. The day had come.

Like one person, they rose up. They had no general, no leader, no governing body. Yet some 12,000 falashas prepared to march from their scattered villages on a long and desperate journey. Among them, in a village in the Wozaga district, were three generations of the Alemie family.*

Three-year-old Tzion, and his sister Orit, five, had watched the skies. Now and then, a distant speck appeared, a plane, and they would race after it. "Stop!" Tzion shouted. "Wait! Take us to Jerusalem."

"Shh," his father, Eigal, said. "It's a secret. No one must know."

To prepare for the journey, the Alemies had sold their few possessions—the two oxen, the sheep, the baskets the women had woven, the ploughshare Eigal had hammered out, even his blacksmith's tools.

"Why are you leaving?" asked a neighbour, a Coptic Christian like many Ethiopians.

"The dryness is coming," Eigal told him.

Indeed, this year the rains had not

*Members of the Alemie family are using their adopted Hebrew names. The events are true, but the identities of the other Ethiopians have been altered for their protection.

come to nourish the land. The crops had been stunted. The cattle had turned pale and scrawny. The famine that had struck Ethiopia was edging northward.

Eigal did not talk to his neighbour about the other reason for his family's flight—persecution under the Marxist government of Lieutenant-Colonel Mengistu Haile Mariam. An American Jewish group had sent a Torah for Eigal's village, but the police had seized and burned the sacred scroll. The Hebrew school was shut down and its teachers were arrested as "Zionist spies." For a time, the police had ordered a village synagogue closed. A month earlier, a man had been stopped on the road and accused of trying to escape to Israel. He was tortured—beaten on the soles of his feet—"so you will not run again."

Eigal had felt trapped. More and more, he thought of the Passover promise: "Next year in Jerusalem." The message of deliverance had been eagerly awaited.

Malka Alemie, 60, the grandmother of the family, entered her *tukul*—a round mud and straw hut with a pointed roof—for the last time. She lit the kindling for her cooking fire and got her batter for *injera*, the flat circle of bread that formed the staple of their diet. Then she gathered her family for a meal—and a prayer: "Our father in heaven, you have made so many miracles. Now we ask you to make one more."

Afterwards, they gathered with the

other families at the village edge. They were simple people with a quiet dignity, and their straight-backed, lean bodies cast shadows in the fading light. When the tender blue of the evening sky turned dark, the 40 villagers began their exodus.

By dawn the next day they had reached a grove of trees. There guides were waiting, gruff men carrying automatic rifles, menacing Russian-made Kalashnikovs slung over their shoulders. They were *shiftas*, bandit gangs that roamed the Ethiopian countryside. Their leader stepped forward. "I am Josef of Armachiho," he told them. Malka's husband, Rahamin, reached under the folds of his *shamma* robe for a knotted bundle of money and paid Josef almost all they had.

From other villages, more falashas came. By nightfall, they had grown into a ragged army of 300 people. Slowly a hushed line of men, women and children moved out. The road was steep, leading them up over a jagged mountain. They walked from sundown to sunrise, stopping only when the daylight made it unsafe to travel. Then they wrapped themselves in their shammas, hid among rocks and trees, and slept.

It was dusk of the third day. When Malka woke she heard one of the guides saying that two smaller groups could move more swiftly, more quietly. Suddenly they were being divided in half. "Quickly, quickly," the guides ordered. "You go here! You go there!"

In the confusion, families were separated. Malka searched frantically as the darkness gathered. "My husband? Have you seen my husband?" But Rahamin was gone, along with two of her daughters, their husbands and children—taken off to follow a separate road to the Sudan.

Malka did not share her foreboding with anyone. All her life, she had been dutiful, first to her father and then to the stranger he chose to be her husband, a good man. *There is no time for tears*, she told herself. Now her duty was to be a *baaltet*, "a wise mother," to whom others, men as well as women, would listen.

"No one else must be lost," she instructed her family. "Resting or walking, we must stay close together." She put the two daughters who remained—one a teenager and the other with a husband and children—at the head of the family column. With them was Avi, aged nine, frightened and weeping for the mother who had been pulled away with the other group. Malka's son Eigal walked alongside the mule that carried little Tzion and his sister. Her daughter-in-law, Kohava, carried their other child, a dozing infant held on her back in an *ankelba*, a babysack made of leather and worn like a backward apron. Malka walked behind them. She did not want them watching and worrying when her body slumped with fatigue and her feet dragged.

That night, as they walked, Malka thought she heard gunfire in the distance. Was it a premonition? She shuddered as she remembered the prophecy of the elders:

"The way will be hard," they had always said. "Not everyone will arrive."

Two nights later, the gunshots were close by. "Down!" the guides shouted. "Get down!" Malka pulled one of her grandchildren from the mule and covered the child with her body. Eigal took the other one.

More shots rang out. It was another group of shiftas demanding money to allow the caravan to pass. The falashas' guides were firing back.

Finally the shooting stopped. "Watch the guides closely," Malka had warned Eigal, because she knew that some guides would let other shiftas stop caravans and go from person to person, collecting money. If someone had no money to give, the shiftas would take a mule, the last sack of food or the person's only pair of sandals.

The bandits were negotiating. "You cannot take money from these poor people," Josef, the guide leader, shouted. "They have paid me and, from that money, I will pay you." He paused and fired a shot in the air. "But only a little."

When they settled on a sum, the caravan moved on. Malka remembered the young messenger, Gideon, who had sent them to this guide. "He was right," she whispered to Kohava. "Our bandit is an honest one."

The road began to grow steeper

and narrower. When it widened again, the guides signalled a halt for a brief rest. Other people had recently followed this road before them; tens of thousands of Ethiopians—Christians, Muslims and Jews—were fleeing the famine and political turmoil. For many miles now, Malka had seen the things those other people had thrown away to lighten their load. Empty water jugs. Worn-out sandals.

Now, in the moonlight, Malka saw something else. An ankelba. The young mother, Kohava, also saw it, and knew. A woman would throw away her baby-carrier only if the baby had died. With a feeling of foreboding, Kohava reached for the ankelba on her own back, stroking the sleeping infant within.

Seeing the terror on Kohava's face, Malka tried to calm her. "No, no," she said. "It won't happen."

The Lost Tribe

THERE are many theories about the origin of Judaism in Ethiopia. Some scholars suggest that it was introduced by traders, missionaries or even prisoners of war by way of the Red Sea. Others believe the story of the falashas began with ancient settlements in Egypt, and a garrison—including Jewish soldiers—on Elephantine Island in the River Nile, near where Aswan stands today. In times of trouble, these Jews trekked south through the Sudan and eventually arrived in the highlands of Ethiopia. There they found green mountains, a temperate climate and a native people, the Agau, whom they converted to Judaism and whose women they married. Scholars have found references to Jews in Ethiopia in Greek writings dating back to 200 years before Christ.

According to Ethiopian tradition, the falashas were descended from Jews brought to their country from Jerusalem by King Menelik, the son of King Solomon and the Queen of Sheba. But in the sixteenth century they were recognized as a remnant of Dan (one of the ten tribes of Israel captured by the Assyrians in the eighth century BC) by the Radbaz, the chief rabbi of Egypt, who decreed: "They are the seed of Israel, of the tribe of Dan, which dwells in the mountains of Ethiopia." It was on this basis that the Sephardi chief rabbi of modern Israel accepted them as true Jews in 1973.

Lost tribe or not, the events that Jews around the world celebrate at Purim and Hanukkah—and Christians at Christmas and Easter—had not yet taken place when Malka Alemie's ancestors arrived in Ethiopia. They had with them only the Torah—the first five books of Moses. Cut off from the outside world, the newcomers had *kesoch*, or priests, rather than rabbis and, unlike other Jewish communities—even the far-flung Chinese Jews of Kaifeng-Fu and the Cochin Jews of India— they had lost the Hebrew language.

Yet in their mountain fastness they guarded their Jewish identity, living apart from their gentile neighbours. Eventually they entered into a cycle of religious wars. In the early seventeenth century, after a terrible slaughter, the Jews were ordered to convert to Christianity. All those who did not become Christians would be *falasai*, strangers who were forbidden to own land. In time the ancient word became falasha.

The falashas resigned themselves to their lot as landless craftsmen and tenant farmers, working the poorest plots and turning most of their crops over to the landlords and the state. It was in this condition of hardship that scholar Joseph Halévy, a French Jew, found them when he arrived in their villages in 1867. Halévy reported: "A traveller with white skin who says he is a Jew—the falashas could hardly believe it."

After the creation of the state of Israel in 1948, the black Jews of Ethiopia sent letters to Jews in Israel, Europe and America, asking for help. But there was no answer until the 1973 recognition of the falashas as Jews by the Sephardi chief rabbi of Israel. Two years later the state of Israel accepted his ruling. This made the falashas eligible for the Law of Return; like all Jews, they could come to Israel to seek citizenship.

But if Israel was willing to let them in, Ethiopia was not willing to let them out. The old "Lion of Judah," Haile Selassie, did not believe in mass emigration. And after he was overthrown by a military coup, the new government, ruled by

Continued on page 150

CROWS FLY THROUGH HOLES WHERE
MAURA LAUGHED.

YOU can't escape the past in Ireland. It's all around you. Sooner or later you'll meet the man who knew someone who was related to Ould Maura of County Clare.

And over a glass and an hour, he'll relate the mysterious fate of her early-departed husbands.

Then, with a wink, turn a haunting to a welcome. You'll find there's a mood to Ireland. Let it take you.

IREL✺AND
YOU'LL ONLY KNOW BY BEING THERE.

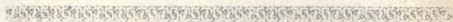

ONCE OULD

a committee known as the Dergue, insisted on closed borders. By the late 1970s, the military regime had become strongly Marxist. The falashas, numbering about 30,000, were harassed by extreme left-wing factions, some of them violently anti-Zionist. Moreover, the Dergue did not allow the falashas to celebrate their holidays openly, or to worship freely. As Jews, they were said to be pro-Israel, pro-American and, in a wild leap, agents of the CIA.

The new laws stirred up old hatreds. In Gonder Province, where the Alemies farmed, the violently anti-Jewish chief administrator blamed the Jews for crop failures. Hebrew, the rediscovered language

of prayer, could no longer be taught. Jews were beaten. Books were burned and houses torched.

Word of these incidents reached Israel. Soon after he became prime minister in 1977, Menachem Begin moved to bring the falashas to Israel—legally if possible. If not, he counted on the agents of the Mossad, the Israeli secret service, to bring them out however they could.

By 1979, there was a small community of Ethiopian Jews in Jerusalem. Some had left as "legal exceptions" to seek medical treatment or to study abroad. Others had stowed away on Israeli ships in the Red Sea and travelled north. A few had been traded to Israel for military equipment. But the *aliyah*—the going-forth to Israel—was hardly more than a trickle.

Searching for alternatives, Begin's advisers studied those countries sharing Ethiopia's borders. Would it be possible, they wondered, for the falashas to make the arduous, 200-mile trek across the mountains and wasteland of Ethiopia to the Sudanese border? As a member of the Arab League, the Sudan considered Israel an enemy. Still, a number of Ethiopian Jews had followed that route, and Mossad agents had helped them on their flight to freedom.

As news of Israeli rescue missions spread, hundreds of falashas did make the trek. Once into the Sudan they took shelter in the sprawling refugee camps near Gedaref, where many thousands of weary, ragged victims of Ethiopia's famine and civil wars had fled. The camps became way stations until the refugees could be moved further along the road to Israel.

A network of refugee groups worked to take them out. Mossad agents shepherded people out of the camps to buses and lorries, boats and planes. In one small exodus after another, often a dozen or so people at a time, some 6,000 in all reached Israel.

But as word of the escape operations leaked out, the risk of an international incident became imminent. Planes were landing illegally in the Sudan. If one was seized or fired

on, there could be repercussions.

Because of this, and because the number of falashas in the Sudan was increasing so quickly, it was clear a bolder plan was needed to remove the refugees from Sudanese territory. But how and when? The answer would be Operation Moses.

Secret Agent

"I KNOW they are hiding somewhere," the Sudanese captain insisted. Even in the blazing summer heat of the dusty, sprawling city of Gedaref, the officer looked dapper in his uniform. He was speaking to the young man who did gardening and odd jobs for him. The captain was fond of this tall and bony fellow, so street-wise behind a lopsided smile.

"Listen, Hassan," the captain said. "Help me to find those black Jews and I'll pay you."

"Black Jews, my captain?" The gardener looked puzzled. "What do you mean? I thought Jews were white."

The young man admired the captain, but he lied to him routinely. He was not "Hassan" and not the Muslim he pretended to be. He was Gideon, a falasha, one of the secret messengers to Gonder.

In his village of Woggera, Gideon had heard of Prime Minister Begin's decision. In 1980, Gideon had been one of the first to make the trek to the Sudan, searching out a route that others could follow. Crossing the border on a return trip, he had been stopped by the captain.

"I am Hassan, a poor Muslim," Gideon began, humbly. "I've come looking for work, as there is none in Ethiopia for Muslims."

"Really?" the captain asked. "How would you like to work as my gardener?" As Gideon nodded, he told him how to reach his house.

At work in the garden, Gideon knew that the captain's suspicion about the Jews in hiding was right. Some were sheltered in the tukuls of Gedaref. Others were in the refugee camps in the countryside. By now, thousands of falashas had crossed into the Sudan. Gideon knew this because he had brought many of them there himself.

As the months passed, Gideon would lie to the captain: "My mother is crying. She wants to see my face." Obligingly, the captain would sign a travel pass to the Ethiopian border for him.

In truth, Gideon's mother was hiding in a tukul near by, supported by her son's wages. And Gideon slipped back into Ethiopia to help those who still waited, as his own father did, for someone to lead them along the secret trails to the Sudan.

Gideon had performed his dangerous mission several times on his own. Lately he had carried messages on behalf of the American Association for Ethiopian Jews, an activist group, zealous and impatient over the falashas' fate. Gideon had heard that the AAEJ pressed legislators in Washington and Jerusalem with such single-mindedness that its members were known as the Crazies or, in kinder moments, the Lone Rangers. They saw themselves as gadflies; whenever they felt Israel wasn't doing enough, they would prod it into action. In Ethiopia and the Sudan, they smuggled money in, and sometimes, staging their own missions, they smuggled people out.

In Gedaref, meanwhile, the Sudanese captain was more than ever determined to ferret out the hidden Jews. "I have it worked out," he told Gideon one afternoon. "The Jews don't light fires on their sabbath, which begins at sunset on Friday. So that night, we shall check to see which houses are dark."

"Very clever," Gideon agreed.

That evening, he hurried along the narrow streets and alleys, spreading a warning from house to house. "You must light a fire this Friday night," he told the falashas. "To save a life, it is permitted. You don't have to use the fire, but *you must* light it."

Although they were working at cross-purposes, the Muslim army officer and the young Jewish falasha grew to be friends. Using English, a language they had both learnt at government schools, they often talked together.

But day by day, Gideon's deception grew harder to maintain. Each week, when the captain invited him to pray at the near-by mosque, Gideon shook his head. Then one Friday, the Muslim sabbath, the captain announced, "No more excuses. Today you're going." With a firm grip on Gideon's arm, he pulled him along to worship.

Inside, Gideon watched the captain carefully, trying to stand or kneel on the prayer rug at the right times. Two or three times, though, he was still bowing on his knees after everyone else was up.

As they walked home, the captain's mouth was a tight, angry line. "You pray like no Muslim I ever saw," he said.

Gideon struggled to keep the fear out of his voice. "It's different in Ethiopia," he tried to explain. "And my family is not religious."

That afternoon, he dug busily in the garden. When he looked up from his work, he caught the captain's stare, suspicious and angry.

Death in the Wilderness

MALKA'S group had been walking out of Ethiopia for eight nights now, moving in the darkness through the mountains, a weary, hungry caravan.

The land was becoming flatter, the days were hotter; they had reached the wasteland—"The desert that doesn't look like a desert," Malka called it. It was flat, with scrub growth, stunted trees and coarse grasses. They had come from the plateau, and the heat of the wilderness made them stagger. Even at night, Malka could feel the hot ground through her sandals. Some people had no sandals, and their feet were blistered.

There were lions in the country, and snakes. A barefoot teenager had been bitten. They had cut the wound and sucked out the poison, but he could not walk. They carried him, delirious, on a stretcher made of tree limbs and strips of cloth.

Their canteens were almost empty, and the guides found one water-hole after another dry. "Soon," they promised. "Soon."

At dawn, after the third night in this wasteland, they approached a spring, gushing with fresh water. There, behind a clump of trees, shif-tas waited for them. Shots rang out and people scattered, flinging them-selves to the ground. In an answering volley, the guides fired towards the trees.

All that day, they laid siege to the water-hole. As the sun was setting, Josef of Armachiho crawled along the ground, reassuring one knot of people, then another. "We and they are old enemies," he explained. "They will not back down; they will not give us water. We will slip away at nightfall."

Malka had come to respect Josef. She thought once again of the young messenger, Gideon, who had recom-mended Josef as their chief guide.

When the night turned black, the falashas managed to get out of range of the guns. They were weak with the heat and dizzy with thirst. Only the guides still had water in the cans that were loaded on their mules. In the middle of the night's walk, they gave each child a small drink.

The next night, Malka heard a moan behind her. She turned to see a tattered skeleton of a man stumble and fall. He lay unmoving on the ground, dead of heat and thirst. In the wilderness, the falashas dug a grave for him. "Hurry!" urged the guides. But there were prayers to say.

The people gathered around the old priest who had come with them and prayed for their lost companion. Then they staggered on in a parched daze.

Later, still days away from the Sudanese border, the travellers were blessed with a night-time rainstorm. The next morning they drank the water that had collected in the crev-ices of rocks.

In two more nights they had passed through the wasteland and into hillier country. "We are coming close to the Sudan," Josef told Malka. "We must say goodbye now, Mama." It was one day's walk to the border, and if the guides were spotted by Sudanese soldiers their guns would be confiscated.

"You are a wise mother," Josef said, smiling. "Take your family straight. You will see three hills. Beyond them is the Sudan."

The Sudanese border guards who met them were bored now by the hordes of refugees pushing into their country each day. Hundreds of thousands had come, fleeing the drought. Christians, Muslims, Jews, they all looked alike, ragged and hungry. Gruffly the guards ques-tioned the newest arrivals. "We are Christians," Malka lied, "running from famine." Eigal then offered the guards money so that the weary family could ride in a lorry rather than walk the last 20 miles.

An hour later, coming over one final hill, Malka could see the teeming acres of tents and tukuls that were their destination—the refugee camp of Um Rakuba. She shuddered. In the heat of the Sudan, the stench of death hung in the air. Not far from the camp a cemetery was growing to the size of a city. After a trek of 17 days and nights, they were still a long way from the Promised Land.

The American Connexion

IN ISRAEL, government officials did not know Malka Alemie's name. Still, they knew what she and a host of others had done. By the summer of 1984, there were more than 10,000 falashas in the Sudan's miserable refugee camps—far too many to be spirited out by the Mossad or by private rescue organizations. A larger-scale operation was desperately needed, and for this the Israelis knew they would require American co-operation.

US State Department meetings to discuss the situation in the Sudan were held in March and April of 1984. Richard Krieger, then associate co-ordinator for refugee affairs, was one of those involved. Krieger and others hoped for a falasha rescue, but knew it could happen only with the consent of the Sudanese Government. And that country had made its anti-Israel position clear. The words of Gaafar al-Nimeiry, president of

the Sudan, were blunt: "Israel knows I am its enemy."

Still, the United States had a certain amount of leverage. Because the Sudan's strategic position on the Red Sea made it a security concern for the United States, and because of America's humanitarian interest in the teeming refugee camps, Nimeiry's country had been receiving more US aid than any other African nation except Egypt.

On a morning in mid-June of 1984, Krieger ushered a Sudanese official into his office. The official wanted more American aid. He ticked off the Sudan's long list of problems—the economic crisis, the Marxist government on its southern flank, the flood of refugees. "And on top of that, those Jews," the man said angrily, "always making trouble."

Krieger nodded, his expression neutral, but with a flash of hope he saw an opening. Playing on his visitor's prejudices, Krieger, himself Jewish, pretended to sympathize. "You're right, and we'd like to help you get those Jews out of your country," he said. "You don't need them making trouble."

Then he dangled the advantages. If the falashas were gone, the Sudanese would have 10,000 fewer mouths to feed. The disturbance of unmarked planes landing on sporadic rescue missions would end—and the "Crazies" would be gone, too.

The Sudanese was smiling, and Krieger lured him on. "If the Sudan is to get more American aid," he continued, "you will need powerful Jewish friends in Washington. Imagine what they could do for your country if they thought you were helping the falashas." It was clear that the Sudanese liked the idea.

Such discussions between government officials eventually resulted in a workable plan. A memo outlining the concept of a falasha rescue was sent to President Reagan and Secretary of State George Shultz. Krieger was dispatched to Jerusalem to brief key Israeli officials. Next, the Sudanese Government agreed to the exodus, but warned that those involved would have to devise a plan that would not embarrass the Sudan in the Arab world.

By September, negotiations had led to a final formula. An international refugee organization would be put in charge of the destiny—and the destination—of the Ethiopian Jews, technically relieving the Sudanese of further responsibility. But to ensure success and protect the Sudanese, this exodus would have to be carried out in total secrecy. No rumours. No leaks.

At last, Operation Moses was under way.

An American refugee official named Jerry Weaver became the US connexion on a planning-and-operations team that included a Sudanese security expert and workers from the still-secret international refugee organization. It had been decided to move the falashas overland from the refugee camps to Khartoum, and by air from there to Israel. Because a fleet of planes would attract too much attention, they would have to settle for one plane-load at a time.

Four bus-loads of people, it was calculated, would fill a plane. Gedaref would be a staging area. Only one good road ran between there and Khartoum. It had a number of police check-points. The problem of getting the buses through was assigned to the Sudanese.

The planes could come to an isolated section of the runway at Khartoum airport from anywhere except Israel, the Sudanese stipulated, flying any other flag. The Sudanese agreed to the airlift only if the planes departed for an intermediate destination before landing in Israel. As a point of logistics, the Israelis argued for direct flights. Then, reluctantly, they agreed.

In late September and early October, at meetings in Geneva, the plans were completed. If all went well, the first rescue plane would take off in a matter of weeks. Yet Jerusalem was alive with rumours and so was Khartoum. Washington leaked like a sieve.

"Can we keep the lid on this one?" asked a worried US official.

"We'd better," another answered him grimly.

"The Answer Is Yes!"

"MY MOTHER is crying," Gideon told the captain. "She wants to see me." One more time, he dared to ask; one more time, his Sudanese friend

Zero interest.
(We predict a rush.)

0% – Free credit on a brand new Metro. That's the sensational low cost finance plan available through Austin Rover Finance.

Put down 30% of the price now and you can enjoy interest-free credit on the remainder, with a full year to pay.

Or if you prefer, for just 20% deposit, credit is only 4.6% (**8.9% APR**) with two years to pay.

There's also a three year payment option. These plans are only available until March 16 so it'll pay to decide now. And beat the rush.

METRO CITY 1.0 3 DOOR		
	Interest Free 0% (0% APR) over 12 Months	Low Cost 4.6% (8.9% APR) over 24 Months
Cash Price*	£4,682.31	£4,682.31
Deposit	£1,404.75 (30%)	£ 936.46 (20%)
Amount of Credit	£3,277.56	£3,745.85
Monthly Payments	£ 273.13	£ 170.43
Charge for Credit	£ 0.00	£ 344.47
Total Amount Payable	£4,682.31	£5,026.78
CUSTOMER SAVING	**£360.53†**	**£479.52†**

METRO

provided a travel pass to the border.

The scrawny young spy, now also working for Israeli agents, was shepherding groups of falashas through the Gedaref alley-ways to rendezvous outside town, where undercover agents waited to take them further.

When Malka Alemie and her family arrived at Um Rakuba, Gideon added their names to his list. His new Israeli bosses wanted to keep track of who and where the Jews were. Gideon could guess why. He could see that scores of falashas were arriving every day. Something had to happen soon.

Before it did, he had one last trip to make, to smuggle a special person out of Ethiopia. "Esther," he sighed, evoking the memory of a graceful young woman with a sweet promise in her smile and plaits in her hair. At 19 she was one of the "old virgins," as people called a new breed of Ethiopian girl who was allowed to go to school instead of being married off as young as 12.

Gideon had never spoken to Esther; he had seen her on only two occasions. Yet some Ethiopians had never seen their intended brides. He did not know whether she cared for him, but he knew he wanted to take her out of Ethiopia—as his wife.

The trip began badly. Crossing into Ethiopia, Gideon climbed the familiar three hills. They seemed steeper than he remembered. He felt dizzy and unsteady. *The malaria*, he

thought. *It's coming back*. He had not escaped the diseases of the refugee camps, but that couldn't stop him now. Shivering with chills and fever, he pushed on.

August, the wet season of Ethiopia, was not quite over. As Gideon walked, the rain drenched him, and it also filled the stream bed. He was moving feebly towards it when a large, tawny animal crossed ahead of him. The youth and the lion spotted each other at the same moment, and both stopped in their tracks.

"Stay still!" a man's voice hissed from behind him. "If you move, he'll kill us both." Heart pounding, Gideon obeyed the voice. For ten minutes, man and beast stared at each other. An eternity of terror passed. Then the lion moved slowly towards the stream and began to drink.

Looking back at the man who had called out to him, Gideon stifled a shout. It was Josef of Armachiho, the Christian guide who was his close friend, the "good bandit" he had recommended to Malka Alemie.

When the lion finished drinking and loped off, the two friends greeted each other. Happily, they filled their water cans and agreed to travel on together.

Gideon struggled to keep up. Dreaming of Esther, he pushed himself hard. A few nights later, when they had reached the Gonder hills, he collapsed. Josef was cradling him in his arms, trying to stop the trembling, when a young Muslim found them.

"Come home with me," the boy insisted. He and Josef carried Gideon on to a small tukul. The boy's family wrapped Gideon in blankets and put him close to a fire.

When Gideon awoke, Josef was watching over him. "Don't sit and suffer here with me," Gideon said. "Go along."

Josef refused, and Gideon smiled at him weakly. "Well then," he asked, "would you be willing to arrange my wedding?" His father was far away in a distant village, Gideon said, but he had an uncle living near by. Perhaps Josef could carry a message, telling Gideon's uncle to visit the village of Esther's family.

"It is the custom," he explained. "My family must visit her family, to ask for the daughter. Tell him I want no dowry. Esther is the only gift I ask for."

"I will come back with the answer," Josef promised. "And if the family is willing, if God is willing, I will dance at your wedding."

For most of the following days, Gideon slept. The Muslim family found some quinine for him, nursed him, fed him. As the days passed, he wondered if Josef had been captured.

"Mama," he told the Muslim woman, "I must go now, too."

"Stay longer," she urged him. "Be our son."

Gideon shook his head. "I will always remember you," he told her.

One by one, he embraced the members of her family. And then he set off. Still weak and unsteady, Gideon was concentrating on the road when a horse came galloping towards him. He looked up to see a rider waving wildly.

"Yes!" Josef was shouting. "The answer from Esther is yes!"

The wedding was to be a traditional one, only faster, everything telescoped by a time of crisis. Two days later, Gideon, Josef and the uncle started out for Esther's village.

There, family and friends had gathered for a wedding feast, a roast sheep, injera, and *tala*, the potent, home-brewed Ethiopian beer. The three men were led to places of honour. A drum and a home-made, banjo-like instrument were playing a pulsing African rhythm.

"Addis Ababa, Addis Ababa," the men sang. The name of Ethiopia's capital, it means "New Flower." To the black Jews, it was a song to be sung at weddings and births, a chant of new hope and a hymn to God. The men danced to it—shoulders shrugging and swivelling, legs leaping quickly back and forth.

Esther was nowhere to be seen as the guests ate and danced. Finally, at a signal from the *kes*, or priest, she was led from the tukul. Her face was hidden by a veil as the white-haired kes read from the Torah. Then Esther and Gideon exchanged promises to be a faithful wife and a good husband. A red-and-white band was tied around Gideon's forehead, a symbol of the bride's virginity and the groom's purity.

As the bride was led away again, the feasting continued. In normal times, it would go on for days. Now it would last only through the night. In the morning, Esther emerged, swathed in a white shamma.

Gideon pushed Josef forward. "Go," he said. "It's tradition." The bride was leaving home and family, and the groom's best friend was now supposed to become her special protector. Josef lifted Esther on to the back of a borrowed horse and walked at her side on the road back to the uncle's house.

Esther and Gideon's honeymoon would be a trek to the Sudan. A few days later, Gideon's uncle loaded a mule with water cans and more food than he could spare. Then he gave Gideon and Esther a special gift: two hard-to-get pieces of paper, the passes that are required to travel from one village to another. "At least your journey will start without trouble," he said.

Million-Dollar Shopping List

WITH his go-ahead from the Geneva meetings, Jerry Weaver moved into high gear. He knew the territory and he had the connexions. He also had the money. Although he wasn't throwing it around, over the next few weeks he would spend a million dollars of Israeli Government money.

Through a broker, Weaver bought fuel for the buses from another Muslim country, and paid 175,000 dollars for it. The fuel was delivered in 55-gallon drums to an abandoned factory that would also serve as an inconspicuous garage. The buses were even harder to find than fuel. Finally Weaver flew to Saudi Arabia, bought four stripped-down lorry frames, and had them shipped to Khartoum, where they would be converted into buses.

Weaver checked and double-checked the route. He shopped for blankets for his midnight passengers, and placed food, water and communications equipment in the quiet house that embassy people used on trips to Gedaref. On the edge of town, just a quick detour from the roads the convoy would be travelling, it could serve as a safe house in an emergency.

The Sudanese were busy, too, checking the condition of the landing-strip at Khartoum airport. Officers were appointed to shepherd the buses through police check-points.

Meanwhile, the Israelis had also gone shopping. They found the planes they needed in Brussels through a charter company called Trans European Airways (TEA). Its president, Georges Gutelman, a Jew, had done discreet business with Israel before. He also had connexions with the Sudan. No one would be surprised to see TEA planes land in Khartoum; they went there regularly to pick up Muslim pilgrims going to Mecca.

On their two-hop route from

Khartoum to Israel, the planes would stop at one of a number of European airports to refuel. In each country, the authorities agreed to the landings, though they were as eager as Israel to keep the story out of the headlines. No one wanted to provoke the wrath of the Arab nations.

Within the borders of Israel, there were cautious preparations. "One day," key immigration specialists were told, "we are going to bring the Ethiopian Jews here." Quietly, space was arranged in reception centres.

Everything was now in place. Just six weeks after the secret meetings in Geneva, the first caravan of buses left Gedaref on November 20, 1984, to race for the plane in Khartoum.

A Place of Death

"WHEN will we go to Jerusalem?" little Tzion would ask.

"Maybe next week," Malka Alemie answered the child at first.

"Maybe next month," she said later.

After a while, the child stopped asking. In Um Rakuba, in that terrible spring and summer of 1984, they no longer knew what day or month it was. For Malka, hope was the next sunrise. "Let us all be alive tomorrow," she prayed.

On a pallet of straw, her son Eigal lay trembling, delirious with malaria. Her daughter-in-law, Kohava, held the baby she had carried out of Ethiopia. For three days, the baby had been shaking, his head burning with fever.

The next day, the baby stopped shaking. At ten months old, he was dead. Kohava's premonition had come true. She remembered the discarded baby-carrier that another grieving mother had left on the trail out of Ethiopia. "Now I will throw away the ankelba," she wept.

The other little children sat outdoors on the ground, too weak and frightened to play. Tzion was now four years old, his sister Orit, six.

Are they going to die too? Malka wondered. On a single day, she counted 20 bodies being carried to the cemetery. She remembered the story of the Exodus out of Egypt when the Jews had despaired. "Is it because there are no graves in Egypt that you have taken us away to die in the wilderness?" they had asked Moses.

In September, American doctors arrived at the camp. Kohava fed Tzion and Orit capsules of medicine the doctors gave her. When Eigal had a second attack of malaria, she gave him quinine pills.

But Malka's nightmare continued. Over the months since the aliyah began, she had asked incoming refugees about her husband and the other family members she had been separated from. Now she heard that they had been arrested by Ethiopian Government troops, then scattered, no one knew where.

TOWARDS the end of November, Malka made her way through the narrow passageways of Um Rakuba, which had become open sewers. She no longer noticed the reek of human waste or the stench of death. Today, as every day, she was going to pick up the flour ration.

Waiting in the queue, she listened to the voices around her. She could hardly believe what she was hearing.

"Those poor Jews," a man was saying. "They are moving them out of the camp at Tawawa."

"They are dying in Tawawa and they will die in another camp," his friend answered. "Why force them to make such a trip?"

Malka wanted to race back to her family, but she made herself walk calmly. If they were moving the Jews of Tawawa, she understood why. Tears were running down her gaunt cheeks but she was laughing, too, as she gathered her family around her.

"The aliyah is starting," she told them. "Yes, yes." She hugged little Tzion to her. "Soon, very soon, we are going to Jerusalem."

And it was true. Gideon appeared the next day and the falashas crowded around him. "Stay here and say nothing," the young messenger told them. "When we have taken the people out of Tawawa, we will come for you." He guessed what they were thinking. "Don't come to Tawawa," he urged. "Be patient for a while longer."

But the Alemie family had waited in the purgatory called Um Rakuba for seven months, and they could wait no more. *What if something happens?* Malka worried. *What if the*

aliyah stops and we are left behind?

At night, pooling their meagre funds with 40 others, they hired a lorry driver to take them the 50 miles from Um Rakuba to Tawawa. In the Jewish section of that camp, there were newly empty huts, and the Alemies moved into one of them.

"Look," Malka said. In front of the hut, a last ember still glowed in the cooking fire. Her voice and hands trembled. "This very night, these people have gone to Jerusalem."

"Such a Nice House"

OPERATION MOSES had begun in confusion.

On November 20, 1984, as the sun was going down, four hired buses made their way across an open field and parked at the edge of the Tawawa refugee camp.

Sudanese security officers fanned out to protect the loading zone. Jerry Weaver watched anxiously as an Ethiopian Jew moved off into the darkness of the camp. The man had been slipped in by the Israelis to help organize the Jews' departure. Quiet and gentle, he also seemed frail to Weaver, who waited as the minutes passed and no one emerged from the camp.

Although he was stronger than Weaver thought, the Ethiopian faced a difficult task. He was supposed to send the most vulnerable people first—the children, the sick and the elderly. But everyone wanted to be saved; everyone wanted to be first.

Wretched scarecrows crowded

around the man, arguing, imploring. Once, in Ethiopia, the falashas had had a quiet dignity. And in the misery and fear of the Sudan, they had waited patiently. But now, stampeded by hope, they became a mob. Shoving and shouting, they pushed past him and ran towards the buses, men and women, mothers with babies, old men with sticks. Weaver tried to hold them back, but they flowed around him and forced their way on to the buses.

"Let's go!" Weaver ordered. The convoy, its buses jammed with refugees, moved out down the Gedaref-Khartoum road. After only a few minutes, they were stopped by a pair of traffic policemen. The headlight of one of the buses was out, a traffic offence. The ranking Sudanese officer hurried from his car at the rear of the convoy. After some discussion, and a look at the officer's identification, the policemen waved the convoy on.

The buses passed through the police check-points with little difficulty. Near Khartoum, they were met by more Sudanese security officers. The convoy was told to wait. Weaver was worried about the delay. If it went on too long, they might be forced to take the people to the safe house and keep them there overnight. In contrast to the near riot at Tawawa, the buses were strangely quiet. Finally they were given the signal to proceed to the airport.

The buses lumbered across the tarmac and came to a stop at the steps of

the TEA's Boeing 707. The first dazed and tattered refugees climbed on board. Some were so weak they had to be carried. Children were crowded three together in some of the seats. Finally, early on November 21, the first plane took off.

The Sudanese authorities were furious. If there was pandemonium like this again, the whole world would learn what they were up to. If it happened again, they said, they would call off the operation.

Two nights later, another attempt was made. There was still confusion, but it went more smoothly than the first trip. The buses arrived in Khartoum almost on schedule. The Sudanese agreed to continue on an every-other-night basis.

Inside the camp, the quiet Ethiopian and list-makers like Gideon struggled for a semblance of order. Moving among the newcomers to Tawawa, Gideon welcomed Malka. In another tukul, he embraced his father, a new arrival from one of Josef's caravans. Gideon's wife, Esther, had been hiding in a tukul at Gedaref. Now he brought her to Tawawa and placed her on one of the buses. She was pregnant, and whatever happened, they wanted the baby to be born in the Promised Land.

As the refugees saw the buses coming back again and again, they began to trust in tomorrow. Before long, the operation was going smoothly enough to shift to a daily schedule of flights. Still, few families left as a complete unit, and

Malka Alemie held her own family back. "Wait, wait," she told them. "We must not be separated. We must arrive in Jerusalem together."

Late one afternoon, Gideon found her. "Gather up your family," he whispered. "When the sun goes down, we will take you all on the bus."

"At last," Malka said, smiling. Her heart pounded with excitement, then fear. As she looked around, she realized that Eigal had gone to the town to buy some food. Little Tzion was nowhere to be seen.

"Don't move," Malka told the rest of the family. She raced down one path and then another, anxiously searching for Tzion. At last, thank heaven, there he was. "Hurry," she beckoned. And finally, as the sky darkened, Eigal returned.

"Quickly, this way," Gideon told them, and the Alemies hurried towards a waiting bus. "Alemie," the list-maker called out at the door of the bus, counting off the family members as they entered.

An excited Tzion peered through the bus window. "Look at those men!" Malka marvelled at the cadre of Sudanese security officers who were guarding the convoy. At each check-point, she held her breath until the four-bus convoy started up again.

For hours, the buses rattled along the road to Khartoum, through the last check-point into the airport. Finally they were at the aircraft steps.

The Alemies were among the first to get off the bus. Malka walked across the tarmac and started up the longest flight of stairs she had ever seen. At the top, she found herself in an amazing place. She was escorted to a big chair, softer than any she had ever known. "Such a nice house," she exclaimed, "but where is the aeroplane?"

Six hours later, the plane touched down smoothly in Europe. The passengers remained on board while the aircraft was refuelled. Then, at about noon, they landed in Israel. As they walked from the plane, many of the people knelt to kiss the ground. Malka knelt too.

"Come," she told Tzion. "Taste the Promised Land. Is it not sweet?"

Deliverance

OPERATION MOSES moved along smoothly, but new refugees were arriving daily in the Sudan from Ethiopia. Gideon met a group at the border one evening to lead them to the Tawawa camp. Then, from the shadows, he heard someone call his Muslim name: "Hassan!"

Gideon turned, startled. He was face-to-face with the Sudanese captain.

"Who are these people?" the captain demanded. "What are you doing with them?"

"They are poor Christians from Ethiopia," Gideon lied, hoping to be believed one last time. "I was telling them that the Muslims of the Sudan will be kind to them."

"Wait here," the captain commanded. He issued orders to two

soldiers, while Gideon tensed, wondering if he would be arrested. Instead, the captain led him and the falasha refugees to a tukul, where they could rest overnight.

At dawn, the captain ordered a lorry to take them to Tawawa. "Is your mother still crying?" he asked Gideon with a small, ironic smile.

"No," Gideon whispered. "Not any more."

Gideon wanted to say he was sorry for the lies. Instead, he held out a hand to his old friend. With his other hand he touched the forearm of the extended one, an Ethiopian gesture of respect and friendship.

"*As-salaam alekum*," the officer said in Arabic. "Peace be with you."

"*Alekum as-salaam*," Gideon responded. "With you be peace."

And Gideon went about his job, unaware that—through no fault of the captain's—Operation Moses was about to crash.

Articles on the airlift had begun to appear at the end of November, first in the United States, then in Israel. Eventually, Israeli officials confirmed the reports. As a result, the Sudan cancelled all flights. On January 6, 1985, the last plane carrying falashas left Khartoum. The aliyah was halted.

Operation Moses had lasted for 47 days, completed 35 missions and rescued some 7,800 people. But hundreds of others had been left stranded in the camps. In Washington, within a week, public and private officials began to lobby for a revival of the airlift.

President Reagan's response was to include discussions on the remaining Jews as part of the agenda of a preplanned visit by Vice President Bush to Khartoum. On March 4, the Vice President met with the Sudanese over tea. By the time Bush left he had an agreement: President Nimeiry would co-operate in an airlift of the remaining falashas—if it was

handled in a different way. It would have to be an all-American rescue and it would have to be handled by the CIA, the only organization that the Sudan trusted to carry it off.

The plans for another airlift—this one called Operation Sheba—were set in motion. On the evening of March 21, the falashas at Tawawa were taken to a remote, red-gravel landing-strip near Gedaref and

divided into six groups. Huddled on the ground, they waited through the hot and gusty night among shrubs and thorn trees that bordered the runway.

As dawn came up on March 22, the first C-130 touched down. Its engines were still running, churning up a cloud of red dust, as the first group of Ethiopian Jews was hurried on board. In less than 20 minutes, it was in the air again.

One by one, the other planes landed, loaded their passengers and took off. Gideon climbed on board the last one. By 9.30, the airstrip was once again deserted. Five hours

In the Promised Land at last: after arrival at the reception centre, the falashas begin adjusting to a new way of life and of worship

after take-off, the planes were landing in Israel.

Tattered and dazed, some laughing, some weeping, many saying prayers, the passengers emerged. The prime minister of Israel, Shimon Peres, was there to welcome the wanderers home.

A few days later, Gideon walked through the bustling streets of Jerusalem with Esther. He gawked at the shops, the traffic, the white faces. Some of them stared back, smiling at the young black couple. "*Shalom*," a soldier greeted Gideon.

"*Mazel tov*," a woman wished Esther, now five months pregnant.

"In this place, they are friendly to strangers," Gideon said.

"In this place," Esther replied with a smile, "we are not strangers."

TODAY there are about 16,000 Ethiopian Jews in Israel. In this remnant of a lost tribe, almost every person has a parent, a child, a brother or sister left behind. Perhaps 10,000 remain in Ethiopia, still murmuring the old falasha prayer: "*Do not separate me, oh Lord, from thy chosen, from the joy, from the light and from the splendour. Let me see, oh Lord, the light of Israel, and let me listen to the words of the just . . .*"   THE END

The land of the Pharaohs?
The world of the Greeks?
Or the sundeck of the Orpheus?

After a hard day's site seeing, what could be more pleasant than relaxing on the sundeck sipping a sundowner as the Mediterranean coastline slips by?

During 1987 Swan Hellenic will be running a wide variety of Mediterranean and Nile cruises, each one an exploration of the artistic, architectural, religious and social history of the ancient world.

We'll be visiting all the more important centres of ancient civilisation, as well as places of general interest like Odessa and Yalta, Morocco and Romania.

Each cruise lasts for 14-17 days, during which we make every effort to keep you in a style to which you could easily become accustomed.

Every cruise is accompanied by a guest lecturer, in fact the 'Orpheus' always has at least four on board, all experts in their field and often a leading authority.

Prices average out at around £100 per person per day.

And wherever you go it is fully inclusive of flights, accommodation, meals, excursions and gratuities.

For full details, simply fill in the coupon below or ring us on 01-831 1234 Ext. 777 (01-831 1515 evenings and weekends).

And find out how to see the Cradle of Civilisation in a more civilised fashion.

Please send me the following brochure(s):   SH/CorC RD 1

Mediterranean Cruises ☐   Nile Cruises ☐

Name _____

Address _____

SWAN HELLENIC
Part of the growing world of P&O.

Send to: Swan Hellenic Brochure Services, Freepost, Eccles, Manchester M30 7JZ.

A MORE CIVILISED WAY TO TRAVEL

HOLIDAY IDEAS '87

You'll find lots of holiday and travel suggestions in the next few pages. When you've decided on the ones you'd like to know more about, turn to page 11, fill in the coupon, tear out the page, fold it as indicated and post it. The brochures will be sent to you through the post.

ITALY
- has everything!

Italy has so much to suit all ages. No other Mediterranean country has such superb sunsoaked coastlines, outstanding scenery, enchanting Mediaeval towns, a wealth of fine art and classic architecture, excellent cuisine and such inviting hospitality.

There's the magnificence of Rome, the beguiling charm of Venice and the elegance of Florence. And for those who want to get away from it all there's the relaxing atmosphere of so many beautiful beaches, inland lakes and romantic islands.

THE ITALIAN
STATE TOURIST OFFICE
1 PRINCES STREET
LONDON, W1R 8AY.

Discover more about Italy — pick up a brochure at your local travel agent and then you will see what we mean when we say —

Italy, so much more to enjoy

HOLIDAY IDEAS '87

Use the coupon on page 11 to get the brochures you want after reading this page.

One of the still-to-be-discovered holiday wonderlands of Europe is **Romania** with its silvery beaches by the sunny Black Sea, spectacular mountain scenery, magnificent wildlife, fascinating art and history, one of the most beautiful of capital cities, Bucharest, and the fabulous Danube river, too. You can discover Romania this year from just £199 for two weeks' full board with flights from Heathrow, Gatwick, Manchester and other UK airports. There are also child reductions and low-rate car hire available. Phone 01-584 8090 Or **60**.

Driving your own car in Spain means you can go wherever you please and take whatever you want with you. The quick, easy way to get there by car is *direct* from Plymouth to Santander with **Brittany Ferries**. This, the only direct ferry service between the UK and Spain, cuts out that long, tiring drive through France. And, during 24 hours on board, you'll enjoy delicious food in the restaurant or coffee shop, maybe see a film in the cinema, relax in a spacious lounge, shop in the Duty Free shop, have a drink at the bar or even dance. There's a nursery and playroom for mothers with very small children and all the cabins are well-equipped and comfortable. In Spain, Brittany Ferries have a splendid selection of *holidays* for you: *Parador Touring* on which you enjoy the freedom of your own tailor-made itinerary; a variety of 7 and 14 night *Car Tours*; self-catering at *Seaside Apartments* in 3 locations within easy reach of Santander; *Short Breaks* from 4 to 9 nights that can show you some of the less known places and popular spots, too; stays at 2 specially selected *Campsites*; and a choice of *Mini-Cruises*. For more information about Spain with Brittany Ferries put **41** on the coupon. Details of their ferry services to and holidays in France **42**.

On land or water at home or abroad enjoy the freedom of doing what you like when you like on **Hoseasons Holidays**. Explore the waterways of Britain or Europe aboard one of 1800 boats or choose from over 7000 Holiday-Homes in 120 locations in Britain, France and Holland. UK Holiday-Homes start from £15 each per week and from £29 for UK Boats and they are all *fully equipped to guaranteed standards*. Ring 0502 87373 for brochure. Or mark the coupon **55** for boats, **56** for homes in the UK; **57** for boats or **58** for homes abroad.

Imagine a holiday company who offered identical holidays to those of their competitors—*but cheaper*. That's the secret of **Tjaereborg**. On average you can expect to pay around 10% less for their package holidays. How do they do it? The answer is that they have no travel agent's commission to pay because *you book direct* with Tjaereborg. And they don't waste money on glossy brochures. What they *do* do is offer a good selection of resorts from the Mediterranean to Barbados as you'll see in their literature. Put **63** on the coupon or phone 01-673 2245.

You've more choice than ever in *Over 60's* holidays at home and abroad with **Saga**. Short breaks, hotel and apartment holidays, University Centres, special interest and coach tours as well as holidays in Africa, Asia, the Americas and Australia—*seven* brochures full! And money-saving ideas include reduced-price extra weeks (and months), single rooms for no extra charge, nightly entertainment at University Centres, discount fares with famous cruise lines, group travel free places and more. Phone 0272 217303 (24 hours) for brochure. Or put **62** on the coupon on page 11.

HOLIDAY IDEAS '87

Use the coupon on page 11 to get the brochures you want after reading this page.

There's a great deal inside your local branch of **A T Mays**—the travel agents. Pop into any one of over 200 branches nationwide and their friendly staff will explain some handsome discount offers on your 1987 summer holiday. For instance there's £20 off per person on overseas packaged holidays booked before the end of February. And there's £30 worth of travellers' cheques free for every passenger booking one of the selected cruise holidays.

A T Mays have other special deals too, such as their Travel Card allowing No Deposit and facilities to help you budget for your holidays; a free cruise and travel bag included in holidays to Australia, and lots more besides.

Among the many other holiday bonuses available are offers such as three weeks for the price of two, free airport parking, free children's places, and many more—full details when you call.

Whatever help you need, whether it's advice on flights, visas, accommodation, insurance or any other holiday or travel query, A T Mays will provide it as part of their *complete travel service*. What's more, reservations are at the touch of a computer button! Look in Yellow Pages for your nearest branch or ring 01 937 5244 or 041 221 0404.

Italy is the country for sun and fun-packed holidays. And no-one knows it better than Italy's leading tour operator, **Citalia**. In their brochure you'll find the very best of Italy whether you want coast, country or city. You can choose hotel or self-catering, fly-drive or own car, fly-coach tours and cruises, 2 or 3 centre and even two country holidays (Adriatic Italy plus Yugoslavia or Sicily plus Malta). Citalia have flights from London, Manchester and Glasgow, a special train from London, or you can travel on the opulent Orient-Express. **43**.

Hire a boat and holiday afloat on the waterways of Britain. Whether seeking adventure or tranquility, fun or nature loving, you'll enjoy a marvellous time. The members of the **British Hire Cruiser Federation** have just the boat for you, too, equipped with hot water, cooker, fridge, shower, toilet and heating for luxurious living afloat. And you'll be surprised at how little it costs. For brochures mark the coupon **36** (Norfolk Broads), **37** (Canals and Rivers), **38** (Scotland), **39** (Cambridgeshire), or **40** (Thames Valley), or phone 0502 62101 *at any time*.

Enjoy the variety of France with **Air France Holidays**. You can choose hotel holidays on the Côte d'Azur, in Provence and Languedoc Roussillon, in Corsica and in Paris; go self-catering in an apartment or mobile home in the sunny south; or take a go-as-you-please Fly & Drive holiday, with or without their recommended hotel accommodation, throughout France and Corsica. Or fly to the French Caribbean and experience French hospitality, culture and cuisine in the tropical sunshine. And all by the scheduled services of Air France. Brochure **31**.

Beautiful bays and beaches, sparkling seas and stunning scenery await you in Holiday **Guernsey**. Set serenely in the bay of St Malo, Guernsey and the neighbouring islands of Herm, Alderney and Sark offer you warmth and complete relaxation. (It's nearly always much warmer here than in the UK.) Getting to Guernsey is easy thanks to a wide selection of sea and air routes and once there, there's accommodation to suit everyone, tempting shopping (VAT-free), superb food and a huge choice of things to see and do. For a free 280-page brochure, put **54** on the coupon on page 11.

When you Ritz it to New Zealand you can stopover and see lots of friendly faces in the South Pacific.

Because Air New Zealand's Round-the-World ticket allows you to stop-over in more South Pacific islands than any other airline. So en-route you can Ritz it to Hawaii, Tahiti, the Cook Islands or Fiji.

And, by taking advantage of our special HOTPAC deals, you can enjoy attractive discounts at some of the best hotels in the South Pacific into the bargain.

As well as our famous Ritz of the Skies in-flight service, your Air New Zealand Round-the-World ticket buys you lots of other benefits too. Like the freedom of the world for a whole year, so you can Ritz it all year long providing you keep heading in the same direction.

Plus, on arrival in Auckland, you've the option of flights onto Wellington, Christchurch, and even Australia.

In fact, there's really a whole world of choice when you Ritz it round the world.

Prices start at £1399. Ask your ABTA travel agent for full details. Or phone Air New Zealand on 01-200 0200.

For reservation enquiries call 01-930 3434.

air NEW ZEALAND
The Ritz of the Skies

Ritz it round the world and see some faces in the South Pacific.

HOLIDAY IDEAS '87

Use the coupon on page 11 to get the brochures you want after reading this page.

Variety is the vital factor in a memorable summer holiday and **Cyprus** is supremely equipped to provide it. Long days of brilliant sunshine, miles of sandy beaches, nature trails through spectacular mountain scenery; and tavernas with charcoal grills, delightful Cyprus wines and waiters liable to break into impromptu dancing displays. In addition to this traditional face of Cyprus there's horse riding, tennis, windsurfing, parascending and more. With its friendly people, excellent hotels and infinite variety, Cyprus is a holiday dream come true. **47**.

CYPRUS

THE ENGLISH RIVIERA
TORQUAY · PAIGNTON · BRIXHAM

Where in England will you find palm trees flourishing? On the **English Riviera**. Here three resorts combine to give you 22 miles of unspoilt coastline and beaches with plenty of elbow room. You'll delight in the stylish seafront, shops and night-life in *Torquay*; enjoy marvellous family fun and great entertainment in *Paignton* and revel in the bustle of a busy harbour and excellent restaurants in *Brixham*. Phone 0803 211211 for a free colour brochure. Or put **50** for Torquay, **51** for Paignton, **52** for Brixham on the coupon on page 11.

If you're taking your car abroad, don't plan anything until you have got the **AA Travel** *Guide to Motoring Abroad '87*. It's immensely helpful whether you're a 'first timer' or a seasoned continental motorist as it tells you about the AA 5-Star Service and provides you with lots of motoring and general information. It also gives details of the AA's ferry and motorail booking services, equipment hire services and their *new computerised overseas routes service* that supplies exactly the degree of detail you order. *Free* from AA Centres, or **30** on coupon.

Crest WELCOME BREAKS

Brighten up your winter with a weekend away. Enjoy a **Crest** *Welcome Break* at any of 45 locations in Britain including London, Bournemouth, Edinburgh and York. Prices are from only £17 per person per night and, in almost every UK hotel, *children stay free in their own room!* Other attractions are Leisure Clubs (3 hotels) and Weekend Hostesses to look after you and your children (19 hotels). You can also take a break *abroad* in several European cities. 2 nights in Amsterdam, by air, cost from £119. UK brochure **45**, Amsterdam **46**. Or phone 0295 67722 or 01-902 8877.

CTC

Here's how to run away to sea *enjoyably!* Sail away from Tilbury on the *Azerbaydzhan* or the *Leonid Brezhnev*—two superb liners on which **CTC Lines** are offering a series of wonderful value cruise holidays. You can enjoy a *Russian Easter* cruise to the Mediterranean, Black Sea and Odessa, flying home via Moscow (9th April for 16 days) from £728; cruise to the *Canary Islands* (11th and 25th April and 9th May for 14 days) from £637; or take the *Apple Blossom* cruise to the Norwegian Fjords (23rd May for 7 nights) from £318. Brochure **48** on coupon on page 11.

DB

Travel is unlimited on the entire German Federal Railway when you have a **Die Bahn** *Tourist Card*. For one incredibly reasonable payment you can spend 4, 9 or 16 days discovering Germany and Austria. A 2nd class Tourist Card costs £55 (4 days), £82 (9 days) or £113 (16 days) or you can choose 1st class at £82, £123 or £170 respectively. You can also travel on some bus and steamer services free. There are inclusive rail holidays (all arrangements made for you) to Germany and Austria, too, that will show you many places that you might miss on your own. Brochure **49** on coupon on page 11.

HOLIDAY IDEAS '87

Use the coupon on page 11 to get the brochures you want after reading this page.

1800 self-catering properties in England, Scotland and Wales are fully illustrated in the **Country Holidays** brochure. They include well equipped cottages, houses and bungalows in the Yorkshire Dales, North Yorkshire Moors, the Lake District, Peak District, Northumbria, Devon, Cornwall, Dorset, Somerset, the Cotswolds, Herefordshire, Shropshire, Norfolk, Suffolk and the south coast counties in England; in all parts of Scotland and Wales, too. Country Holidays also operate an instant booking service. Ring 075 678 776 for a brochure or **44**.

What better way to start your holiday in Jersey or Guernsey (and to finish it) than by 'cruising' there and back with **British Channel Island Ferries**. You can sail by night, any night, or by day, any day, from Portsmouth *all year round* and, from May 15th to September 26th, by day from Weymouth. The return fare for adults is from only £38 (that's a 5-day return) and you can take your car with you from as little as £46 return. There are also lots of mid-week travel bargains for families. Both Jersey and Guernsey have their own special holiday magic that British Channel Island Ferries can help you to enjoy to the full with a big new range of all-inclusive holidays. You can choose from hotel, guest house and self-catering holidays in the Islands—all of them offering outstandingly good value. Both islands have their own special appeal and both offer you stunning scenery, VAT-free shopping, delicious food and more than a hint of France. Get full details of British Channel Island Ferries sailings and their programme of inclusive holidays in Jersey and Guernsey by putting **34** on the coupon on page 11 now.

Martin Rooks Holidays

During 30 years of 'direct selling' **Martin Rooks** have built a unique reputation for value and variety. In this year's programme, their biggest ever, they offer over 200 hotels and apartments in over 100 different resorts throughout Europe, flights from 7 UK airports and generous discounts for children—as much as half price! No wonder so many holidaymakers choose Martin Rooks again and again. Get your Martin Rooks brochure by phoning 01-460 6000 now (or put **61** on the coupon, page 11 then book your holiday *direct* either by post or by phone.

Fly to Canada's west coast for the holiday of a lifetime in **British Columbia**. This is the province that offers you the biggest holidays in Canada, bustling cities including Vancouver, 370 parks, the highest waterfall in North America, the Rocky Mountains, some of the world's most breathtaking scenery, the Pacific Coast and more. You'll see the very best of it on a National Holidays coach tour, from £895. And who better to get your holiday off to a flying start than Air Canada who fly direct to Vancouver from Heathrow. Brochure **35** on coupon.

Ask anyone who's been there what they can tell you about **Jersey** and you'll find it hard to resist: the variety of things to do—indoors and out; the picturesque countryside, clean seas and marvellous beaches; the opportunities to enjoy your own sport or try out a new one; the double pleasure of an excellent meal and not adding VAT to the otherwise reasonable bill; plus, of course, the atmosphere—a unique island blend that's undoubtedly French yet unmistakably British. For more about Jersey call 01-200 0200 or put **59** on the coupon on page 11.

Scot free

"Sun streaks the great mountains with gold, as Queen Victoria and her consort gaze across royal purple heather to their Balmoral home . . ."

The freedom of Scotland - past and present - is yours. And getting to know Queen Victoria's 'Dear Paradise' won't cost the earth. In fact, our brochures won't cost you a penny.

We'll send you up to six colourful guides, bringing you closer to majestic mountains, silver sands, silent lochs; all the romance and history of bonnie Scotland. They're packed with helpful hints on where to stay, with details and addresses of hotels, traditional B&Bs, self-catering accommodation, campsites and caravan parks. Choose your six brochures now - scot free.

Scotland's for me!

RD2

1.	South West Scotland	12.	Perthshire
2.	Scottish Borders	13.	Loch Lomond, Stirling & Trossachs
3.	Ayrshire & Burns Country	14.	Fort William & Lochaber
4.	Cunninghame	15.	Isle of Skye & SW Ross
5.	Argyll & The Isles	16.	Ross & Cromarty
5a.	Dunoon & The Cowal Peninsula	17.	Inverness, Loch Ness & Nairn
6.	Greater Glasgow	18.	Aviemore & Spey Valley
7.	Scotland's Valleys	19.	Angus
8.	East Lothian	20.	Grampian Highlands & Aberdeen
9.	City of Edinburgh	21.	Caithness & Sutherland
10.	St Andrews & NE Fife	22.	Orkney
11.	City of Dundee	23.	Shetland

TWENTY-FOUR FRIENDLY DESTINATIONS TO EXPLORE.

Choose up to six areas and discover romantic Scotland. Check the numbers with the map above and tick the six areas you have chosen. Please send me six Scot free guides.

Name _____

Address _____

Postcode _____

Date _____ / _____ / _____

Scottish Tourist Board LONDON SE99 6TT Telephone 01-691 9000

HOLIDAY IDEAS '87

You'll find lots more holiday ideas on pages 171, 172, 174 and 175. When you've read them all and decided which brochures you want sent to you, fill in the coupon on page 11 and post it. They'll be sent to you by post by the various holiday and travel advertisers.

For unbeatable value, places to stay, family fun and a fabulous nightlife, head for **Blackpool**. Choose from a wide range of affordable accommodation and enjoy entertainment that won't make a hole in your pocket! **32**.

Top of the UK's 1986 sunshine league, **Folkestone, Hythe** and **Romney Marsh** are the perfect holiday choice. Mini-breaks including day trips to France start from only £33. For a free colour holiday planner phone 0303 44836 (24 hours). Or **53**.

Lively action and every attraction is to be enjoyed in **Bridlington**—the place that makes the most of Yorkshire's holiday coast. New this year is *Leisure World*, an undercover play area that includes an outdoor 'beach' indoors. It's just *fun*tastic! **33**.

There's *Moor to enjoy* in **Yorkshire and Humberside**. 100 miles of beautiful coastline, historic cities and lush dales. Phone 0904 707961 for the Yorkshire & Humberside guide 70p. Or **64** on coupon page 11.

Use the coupon on page 11 to get the brochures you want after reading this and all the other Holiday Ideas pages.